MICHAEL SWA[...]

THE
EAST INDIAN
KITCHEN

Enduring Flavours of Maharashtrian-Portuguese
Fusion Cuisine

westland

THE
EAST INDIAN
KITCHEN

westland ltd
Venkat Towers, 165, P.H. Road, Maduravoyal, Chennai 600 095
No.38/10 (New No.5), Raghava Nagar, New Timber Yard Layout, Bangalore 560 026
Survey No. A - 9, II Floor, Moula Ali Industrial Area, Moula Ali, Hyderabad 500 040
23/181, Anand Nagar, Nehru Road, Santacruz East, Mumbai 400 055
47, Brij Mohan Road, Daryaganj, New Delhi 110 002

First published by westland ltd 2011

Text Copyright © Michael Swamy 2011
Photographs © Michael Swamy & Pravin Pol
Sketches and Paintings © Philip D'Mello & Eustace Fernandes

All rights reserved

10 9 8 7 6 5 4 3 2 1

ISBN: 978-93-80283-38-8

Food Stylists: Michael Swamy & Mugdha Savkar
Design: Supriya Saran

Printed at Manipal Press Limited

Contents

For
Family &
Good Friends
Aunt Clarice, Pinky Chandan,
Mugsy & Johann

Acknowledgements

The completion of this book was greatly helped by the support of friends and family, lovely people, several of whom are not here in Mumbai. They have moved on and away. I owe special thanks to them — some living, and some no more. Ethel Rodricks da Silva, Clarice D'Souza, Doris Henriques, Blanche D'Silva, Elsie Nunes, Julie Gonsalves, Neela D'Souza, Sylvia Martin, Joyce Esperance da Fonseca (Portugal) and Edith Esperance, Fay Pereira and Fr. Larry Pereira.

I am grateful to artist Eustace Fernandes and friends Pinky Chandan and Angelique Kriplani who helped in several ways. Some of Pravin Pol's food images have gone a long way to make the dishes even more exciting. My ventures into Vasai (Bassein) and other East Indian villages were greatly enriched by the presence of Reynold Dias and family, Bernard Baptista (Vasai), and Svarida Baptista (Matharpakadi).

Artist Philip D'Mello (Vasai) has with great generosity, permitted the reproduction of his paintings. A thank you to Deepthi Talwar of Westland Ltd. and Sherna Wadia for their support and help in the completion of the book.

At home in Prabhadevi, recreating some recipes, cooking, tasting and food styling for the photographs, were shared with and assisted by Angeline Fernandes and Mugdha Savkar. Their contribution has been invaluable.

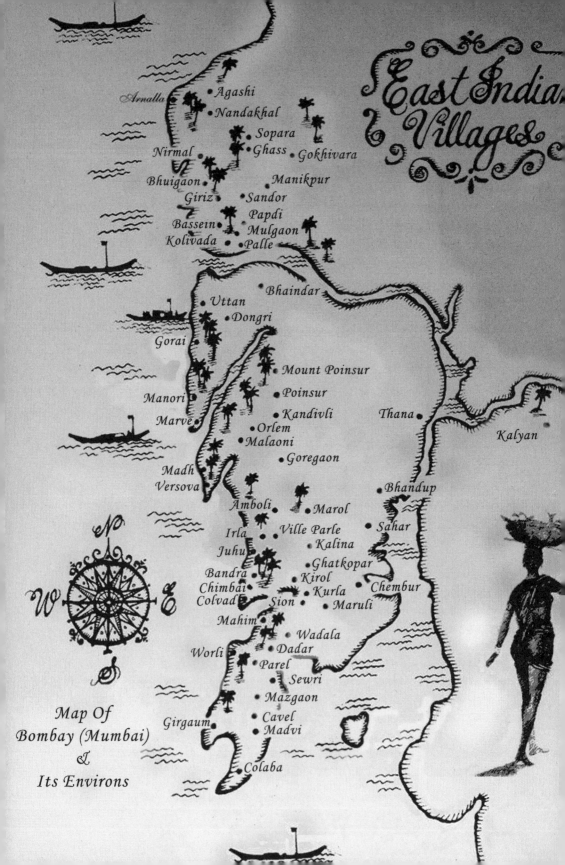

Foreword

History is the essence of innumerable biographies.

Thomas Carlyle, 1795-1881

In pursuit of *Enduring Flavours*, we set out early one Sunday morning from Prabhadevi, for Vasai. From D'Silva Wadi, once a small coconut-palm-dotted East Indian bastion, we took a nostalgic trip away from dilapidated, battered maximum Mumbai. At Holi Digha village, Reynold Dias guided us to the family home. We got out of the car somewhat short of the main house and had a fortuitous brief encounter with a genuine native. Concu Diego Dias was coming home from Sunday mass decked in her red lugda, white vole and traditional gold jewellery. Her house was diagonally across from Reynold's. Michael took his first picture and our visit to Vasai seemed full of promise.

Reynold Dias and the family greeted us warmly: Catherine Falcao his wife, his sons, Regan and Riborn, and Mary Kulas Joaquim Dias (seventy-six), Reynold's mother. Grandfather Inas (Ignatius) Dias was a carpenter. (Some of his hand-made furniture is stacked in a small room; an ideal stash for would-be raiders.) Inas had three wives. The first gave him five daughters; the second, two sons and a daughter; and the third gave him a son and a daughter. Those were the days of large families when farming and fishing were hard, but living was, so to speak, easy.

We then set out for Naigaon, past the Pali Church to meet boat-builders Xavier (fifty-six) and Leslie (fifty) D'Mello, who with thirteen workers, were building a beauty. Their order was for a vessel for Chandraka Nakhwa — Koli. The work began in October. It takes almost six months to put the fishing vessel together at a cost of about Rs 25 lakhs. The wood comes from Gujarat in twelve-ton lorry loads, with a total requirement of thirty-five to forty tons per boat. The workers are from Gujarat and Vasai. The D'Mello brothers receive two to three orders a year. We set out on our mission to visit and revisit the great sights and as many churches as we could make time for — St. Michael's (Manikpur), St. Xavier's (Giriz), Our Lady of Remedy.

The Bassein fort, in the lush and overgrown splendour of its ruins, was as enticing as it always is when one wanders from ancient college to church (fourteen of them) to history-telling graveyards. The afternoon sun was strangely soft and mellow in the enclosed quiet. We could see from Fort Kolivada across the water to Bhayendar and Uttan at Pachu Bunder. The scent of salt fish and sea air was carried by the brisk breeze. Now it was time to turn and head back from the lush over-growth of a decadent past to the bollywooded highways of a dying metropolis.

Michael's pursuit of the enduring flavours of East Indian cuisine is in fact a personal search for the essence of innumerable biographies, of roots and of local history. Given his name Michael Fernandes Swamy, it is intriguing that my great-grandfather should be buried under the name of Michael Fernandes at St. Andrew's Church, Bandra. Did the archangel Michael reincarnate as surgeon and then as chef, writer and food stylist? Each recipe in this book must obviously go back to one particularly creative cook, and then down the ages, yielding to the imagination and initiative of distinctive communities or daring newcomers, emerging, essence intact, as yet another invention.

Jane Swamy

The Purpose and Pursuit

I n more ways than one, this book is a close personal look into a culture and cuisine I was brought up on. Not being born an East Indian, I grew up under the protective wing of my mother's family, which is East Indian. A chef by training, and having cooked and tasted a variety of cuisines, I am curious about fusion, the intermingling and the connection of styles and taste.

Indian cuisine itself is a rich fusion dating back to the time of the Buddha around 600 BC. Over the centuries, traders and invaders came from Greece, Italy, Persia, the Middle East and the Caribbean Islands. The Chinese, Arabs, Mughals, Portuguese and British have come and gone, both giving and taking, by way of fair exchange or loot, and our Indian heritage was enriched by the range in taste, in variety and diversity.

Commodities exchanged with other nations included spices, indigo, silk, cotton and sugar. Cinnamon and cassia came from Sri Lanka. The Arabs brought mustard, fenugreek, cumin and coffee. Arab traders also brought in the banana. Coriander came from China and Middle Europe, hot chilli peppers from the Caribbean and saffron from the Mediterranean. It would seem impossible to imagine Indian cooking without the chilli, brought by the Portuguese from the West Indies. By 1542, three separate varieties of chilli grew in India. Around the sixteenth and seventeenth centuries, the Portuguese introduced the potato, cauliflower, okra (bhindi), pineapple, papaya, cashew nut, and most importantly the tomato, which created a huge impact on the cuisines of India. The spices, vegetables and fruits transplanted during the sixteenth century adapted well to Indian soil.

East Indian cuisine is rich, flavourful and especially appreciated at weddings and on Christian feast days. More often than not, however, getting recipes from members of the community is a daunting task for the faint-hearted, family connections notwithstanding. Families guard their recipes closely and seldom have them written down. Mothers pass them on to favourite daughters and rarely to daughters-in-law.

Oral tradition and fine-tuning also led to piquant niceties in the eventual recording of recipes, aided by my grandmother Ethel Da Silva's collection and E.E. Nune's. So stumbling on, between tasting, testing and recording or redoing recipes, I was able to enjoy interesting new relationships and understand East Indians themselves much better.

One of the numerous reasons for embarking on this project was to combine history with cuisine to uncover culinary secrets and appreciate the community and their cooking talent and bring it all in the public domain. The collection of recipes offered here comes from family and friends.

There are several recipes in the book which are familiar and can be found in other publications, such as frithad or khuddi, which cannot be left out. They are essential in the East Indian culinary range, known to almost every genuine East Indian chef. I have slightly modified several recipes in order to create a type of nouvelle cuisine. I have also included a few Portuguese ones. Working on the book between jobs has been a bitter-sweet affair to remember.

Michael Swamy

Table of Measures

1 cup = 250 ml			1 tbsp = 3 tsp		1 tsp = 5 ml
Oven Temperatures					
Fahrenheit	Celsius	Description	Fahrenheit	Celsius	Description
225	110	Cool	250	120	Cool
275	140	Very low	300	150	Very low
325	170	Moderate	350	180	Moderate
375	190	Hot	400	200	Hot
425	220	Hot	450	230	Very hot

Mumbai

I t was on March 27, 1668, that the islands of Mumbai, earlier called Bombay, were given to the British East India Company at a rent of £10 per annum by King Charles II. King Charles II had received Mumbai as a dowry when he married the Portuguese princess Catherine de Braganca. Mumbai became the headquarters of the Company from 1672-1858 AD. (In 1818 AD, the Company came under the Crown's rule.) The British decided to remove Portuguese clergy and expelled them in 1770 AD. The Carmelite Fathers of Surat were invited to take charge of Mumbai's churches, thereby starting the Ecclesiastical Province of Bombay and its dependencies.

The island of Mumbai at one time comprised seven tiny islands joined together by reclaiming land over the last few centuries (Colaba, Mazagaon, Old Woman's Island, Wadala, Mahim, Parel, Matunga and Sion). Mumbai was once part of Emperor Ashoka's empire. The islands were ruled by a succession of Hindu kings till 1343 AD, when the Mughals took over Gujarat and ruled for the next two centuries.

When Mumbai, Bandra, and the remainder of Salcette were handed over to the Portuguese, numerous churches were built. From 1570-1600 AD, several villages converted to Christianity. The only church standing is St. Andrew's in Bandra. Another large church, in Dadar, was pulled down in the 1980s to make way for a grander, modernised church now known as Salvation Church but still referred to as the Portuguese Church.

Mumbai has its fair share of ruins to boast of, including the remnants of bastions at Sion, Mahim and Bandra. In disrepair, they are a silent testimony and home to the homeless. Called 'Bom Baia', the Portuguese term for 'Good Bay', the islands were later named Mumbai, after the Koli Goddess Mumba-devi, whose temple stands at Babulnath, just off the famous Chowpatty beach.

The Kolis are the earliest settlers on the island and remnants of their settlements can be seen in areas like Colaba, Matharpakadi, the dock areas, Bandra, Madh Island and Gorai. The community is an industrious one, and though simply clad, they bedeck themselves with gold necklaces, earrings, anklets and bracelets. Although modern city life has crept into the community, the Kolis maintain their identity. Koli life once centred on fishing and maintaining nets and boats. The other old inhabitants of the islands are the Bhandaris (distillers and toddy tappers), who brewed liquor from palm or rice. The swampy nature of the islands also enabled the Bhandaris to cultivate rice, vegetables and fruit.

The local Christians foresaw considerable change in their standing by way of government appointments and nominations to Parliament. Moreover, to prevent the British from confusing them with Goans, Mangaloreans and other Christian identities, the community along the upper west coast decided to adopt a new designation. On the occasion of the Golden Jubilee of Queen Victoria (February 16, 1887), the Queen of England and Empress of India, the Christians of the north Konkan adopted the term 'East Indian', primarily to impress on the British and the Crown that they were the earliest Christians of the soil. Though they were geographically incorrect in adopting this nomenclature, in another way they were right in doing so. According to early European and Church geography, a part of the world was divided into the West Indies and the East Indies.

The East Indians then formed The East Indian Association whose principal purpose was, and still is, to protect the economic, social and vested interests of the community. At the same time, the Goans declared themselves loyal to Portugal and to the Archbishop of Goa at a mass meeting in Mumbai (1888) at the Sir Framjee Cowasjee Institute situated opposite the Metro cinema.

This decision of the East Indian community stood them in good stead, for soon Mumbai became the British base. On April 16, 1853, a twenty-one-mile long railway line, the first in India, was opened between Mumbai's Victoria Terminus and Thana. It was only around 1860 that Mumbai saw fresh piped water from Tulsi, Virar and Tansa lakes. Till 1860, water was obtained from wells.

The Gateway of India was built to commemorate the visit of King George V and Queen Mary for the Durbar at Delhi in 1911. The island of Mumbai is a port unrivalled by any other along the coast of India and the British took full advantage of this. The major part of the east coast of Mumbai was made into docks — Mazagaon and Colaba. All the comings and goings soon made the city the financial capital of the country. The departure of the British in 1947 brought more changes. Many of the East Indians had fought in the Quit India Movement but strove to maintain their East Indian identity.

BANDRA

Bandra is a very fine village comprising more than 20 hamlets or pakhadis.

Fr Gomes Vaz, 1576 AD.

Once known as 'The Queen of the Suburbs', Bandra has changed almost beyond recognition. From paddy fields to concrete jungles, the charm that once was has disappeared — including name changes from the Marathi 'Vandra' to the Portuguese 'Bandora' to Bandra by the British.

From the time of the Portuguese, till 1732, there were the villages of Chuim and Candeli near Chuim. Rajan, Sherly, Malla, Palli, Parvar (near Khar Gymkhana; extinct after 1853), Old Kantwadi (now called New Kantwadi), Ranwar, Boran, Tanque (Tank), Patarvar, Santa Cruz, Khar, Cumbarvara, Catirvara near Khar and Povoacao all made up Bandra. The area was covered with rice fields, coconut groves and vegetable gardens, and these were its main exports.

The first oratory to be built in Bandra at the top of the hill is the renowned Mount Mary by the Jesuits, around 1566-1573. A century later, this chapel was razed to the ground

by the Marathas and the statue of Our Lady of the Nativity was flung into the sea. It was later rescued by fishermen and taken to St Andrew's; it was brought back to the mount when it was rebuilt in 1761. The oratory building gave way in the early twentieth century to the present Gothic-style church, built in 1902 and completed by 1904.

Bandra, by 1616, had around 6,000 Catholics whose parish church was St. Anne, standing south-west of the present Bandra station, and next to the present BEST depot. The church stood facing St Michael's on the other side of the creek. At the time considered one of the most beautiful of all the churches built, it has a large number of parishioners. Owing to this, the new parish of St. Andrew was formed. On March 25, 1739, the British destroyed the church of St. Anne to prevent the advancing Marathas from using it as a fort to attack them across the Mahim creek. The monolithic cross at St Andrew's and the baptismal register from 1715 onwards (preserved at St. Andrew's) are what remain of old St. Anne's.

The converts in Bandra were drawn from among the Kunbis (cultivators), the Bhandaris (toddy tappers) and Kolis (fishermen). St. Andrew's was originally built by the Kolis for their community in Mumbai. Many converts took the surname Gomes as they were baptised by Jesuit Brother Manuel Gomes. Some retained their old names and one researcher has established that at least twelve families in Bandra still use their former Hindu surnames, especially those of the Koli and Bhandari communities.

ST. ANDREW'S

In 1965, the façade of the church was demolished and a new one, a replica of the old, was put up. The sixteenth century pulpit, beautifully carved in the shape of a flower whose seven petals are held together by angels, still stands. The other historic relic at St. Andrew's is the wooden statue of Mary with the child Jesus (Our Lady of Navigation). An interesting aspect to St Andrew's Church is the sky-light just above St. Andrew's statue. Its purpose is to let the sun shine through the church on to the keystone separating the sanctuary from the main altar. This phenomenon happens twice a year on the days of the Vernal Equinox (March 21 and 22) and the Autumnal Equinox (September 22 and 23).

MAZAGAON & MATHARPAKADI

The little village off Mazagaon, as mentioned earlier, is another stronghold of the East Indian community. Situated at the eastern end of Mumbai, the word Mazagaon means 'my village'. This tiny village still houses much of the East Indian community. Mazagaon area was leased by the East India Company to Alvares Pares da Tavora for Rs 750 per annum in the early seventeenth century. Mazagaon once had groves of mangoes and is said to be the birthplace of the Alphonso mango. Much of the village of Matharpakadi still houses some of the old buildings of Portuguese design with tiled roofs and balconies. Traditional festivals like the Novena and Feast of the Holy Cross are celebrated on May 1 each year culminating in the Cross feast on the last Sunday of May. The cross in the centre of the village of Matharpakadi was erected by the villagers in 1875 as thanksgiving for the end of the deadly plague of 1870.

THANA (THANE)

Thane is situated to the north of Mumbai, and as part of the mainland, is separated from the other islands by the Thana creek. This city as it now stands has been known by a whole gamut of names: Chersonesus, Shri Sthanaka, Puri, Tanna, Tana Mayambu, Cacabe de Thana and Thana to name a few.

Thane had a great reputation as a port for the export of leather, incense, buckram and cotton. Prior to the reign of the Portuguese, it was under the rule of King Tanamayambu of Gujarat as noted by Duarte Barbosa, a traveller and writer during the fifteenth century. Till the arrival of the Portuguese in these parts (1530-1739), it was known as Cacabe de Tana and was divided into eight pacarias. Home to some rich Portuguese, there were grand villas all along the creek.

Parts of the old Thana fort date back to 1078 AD. The Portuguese lost it to the Marathas in 1739 who ruled over it till 1784. The fort then fell into the hands of the British who made Thane the district headquarters for their administration. Near the fort is the church of St. James built by the British in 1825. Now an independent city, Thane has changed with the modern era and has very little left to show of its past.

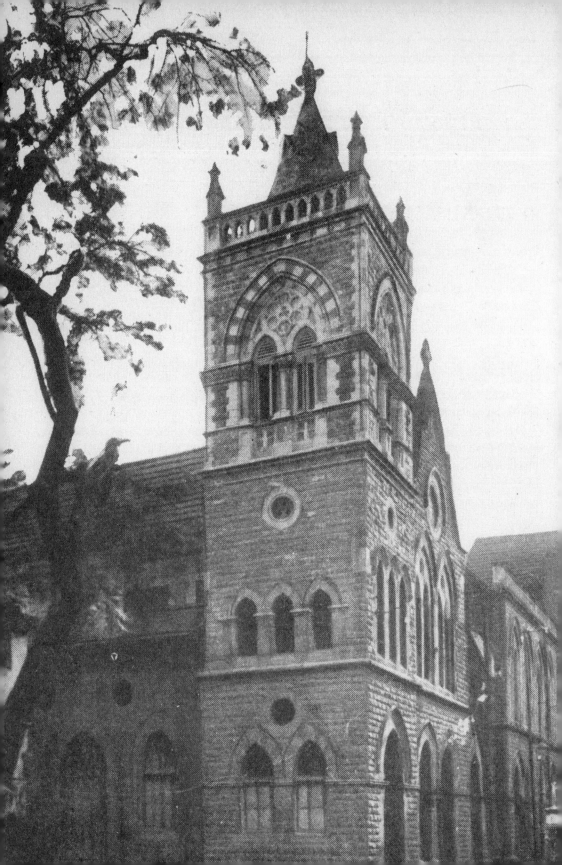

THE EAST INDIANS

Ⓔast Indians, as a designated community, emerged in 1887. The origin, however, of Christians in North Konkan is said to go back to the first century AD.

To understand East Indian cuisine, one must delve into their origins as a people and into their culture. The East Indian Community was officially recognised in 1896, but that was not the year of its origin. East Indians are indigenous to the west Konkan coast of India and owe their nomenclature not to natural growth but to a change of religion. Their ancestors were the Marathi-speaking people of what is now Greater Mumbai and its environs (north Konkan).

India was introduced to Christianity long before England (St Augustine, 579 AD) and Ireland (St Patrick 432 AD). Modern research indicates that the Gospel was first preached in north Konkan by St Bartholomew, one of the twelve Apostles of Christ. (Eusebis 265-340 AD, father of church history and an authority on biblical geography) and (Rufinus of Aquil 345-410 AD). This evangelisation resulted in the formation of an organised Indian Christian community, and is evidenced by Kosmos Indicopleustes in the sixth century AD and Jordanus (Bishop Jordan Catalani) who laboured among the Christians in the Thane and Sopara (Vasai) districts in the fourteenth century (1323 AD). Most of the other Christian communities were based at Kalyan, Chaul (Revdanda). This fact is acknowledged by Pope John XXII, in 1329 AD in his letters to the Christians of the area.

In north Konkan, the Christians were under Muslim rule subsequent to the defeat of Rama Deva by Ala-ud-din Khilji, Emperor of Delhi, in 1294. Temples and churches in the area were destroyed by Mubarak Shah, who in the local tradition, was described as Mumba Rakshasa (demon). The Muslim headquarters was based at Thane and it was here, in 1321 AD, that four Franciscan missionaries were martyred by the Muslim governor of Thane. Under Muslim rule, the Christian strength diminished and the Indian church witnessed a likening to the European Dark Ages (from the ninth to the fourteenth century). Without the existence and support of priests to administer the rites of their religion, they were soon reduced to a nominal status outside the Hindu fold. It was not till the arrival of the Portuguese in India that Christianity in the region grew once again. Some scholars write that: 'It would be a mistake to assume that the Portuguese introduced Christianity to the north Konkan, as many professing the faith were descendents of the old community who had preserved their faith.' Nevertheless, it appears to be more historically correct to accept that when the Portuguese arrived by sea to trade, they did in fact, through their missionaries, achieve the Christianisation of several thousand natives. They were ignorant of the fact that they were coming to a land of venerable antiquity. They were totally ignorant of the presence of the Buddha in India, or of St. Thomas and St. Bartholomew in the north Konkan.

By 1510, the Portuguese had control of Goa and were soon building forts along the coastline to control and oversee maritime trade across the Indian Ocean. Goa was captured by Alfonso de Alberquerque from the Sultan of Bijapur and made into a Portuguese stronghold. By around the sixteenth century, the Portuguese had control of the south, north Konkan (1534), Goa, Daman, Diu and the Malabar coast. Thus, whilst we cannot be certain about the conversion of the East Indians in the early period of the first century AD, there are sufficient records to trace that connection to between 1547 and 1600 AD.

During those years, several villages accepted the Catholic faith, in north Konkan from Dahanu in the north to Chaul in the south. This conversion and the foundation of the East Indian community were mainly due to the zeal of the Franciscans and Jesuits. Two missionaries whose work was outstanding at this time were Fr. Antonio do Porto O.F.M. and Bro. Manuel Gomes s.j.

BASSEIN FORT

The long-standing Portuguese-East Indian bond is best witnessed in the ruins of the Bassein fort, fifty kilometres north of Mumbai at Vasai, the Bahadarpur of the Muslim rulers, the Dom Bacaim of the Portuguese, the Bajipur of the Marathas and the Bassein of the British. At that time, Bassein encompassed the areas of Thane, Kalyan and Chaul. Bassein was an important centre for trade long before the arrival of the Portuguese in 1528. Captain Hector de Silveira, a Portuguese officer, burnt and razed the city to the ground in 1532 AD.

With large mud flats, Bassein was rich in agriculture — cotton, betel, sugarcane — salt, fish, timber and basalt. It was a major port for the arriving Arabs, Greeks, Romans and Persians, who traded in horses in return for spices. The signing of the treaty between the Portuguese and the Sultan on December 23, 1534, gave them control of Bassein and its dependencies in Salcette, Bombaim (Mumbai), Parel, Vadala, Siao (Sion), Vorli (Worli), Mazagao (Mazgaon), Thana (Thane), Bandra, Mahim and Caranja.

With the arrival of Saint Francis Xavier in 1548, Christianity flourished and by 1606 the Portuguese had built nine churches at Nirmal (1557), Remedi (1557), Sandor (1566), Agashi (1568), Nandakhal (1573), Papdi (1574), Pali (1595), Manikpur (1606) and Merces (1606) in the Bassein area. In addition to churches, Western education was brought to the populace with two colleges being built by 1674.

The Bassein fort stands much in ruins today, but was a bastion at the time. Its ramparts surrounded the entire city by the end of the sixteenth century. The remains of several old churches in the precincts include St. Anthony's near the Land Gate. One of the most distinctive features is a thirty-seven-foot-long flying arch at a height of twenty-one feet, which spans the entire width of the nave and is still intact. St. Anthony's was constructed around 1557 by the Franciscan religious order, the first missionaries to come to Vasai. Gonsalo Garcia (1557-1597), the only Indian Catholic canonised as saint was a Franciscan. He grew up in the neighbourhood of yet another church in Bassein fort. Under the Portuguese, the area flourished to the extent that the Portuguese minted their own currency in the 'Casa da Moeda' (Castle of Money).

The Portuguese gave generously to Christian converts by way of land, economic privileges and political office. Those in close contact with them grouped themselves into a seemingly casteless society, accepting Portuguese as a part of their language. The Christians in the rural areas and fishing folk were treated with indifference. They were denied education, but were allowed to retain their ancient culture.

The influence of the Portuguese East India Company and the Dutch East India Company extended over the coasts of India, Sri Lanka and the Moluccas. In December 1600, the British East India Company was chartered, and competition became keener. The British concentrated on the Indian subcontinent and established a base in Surat (1612). Between the fall of the Portuguese and the rise of the British, the Marathas were on the scene for nearly half the century. They focussed on ousting the Portuguese but were tolerant of native Christians.

So it was, till the nineteenth century. The gifting of Mumbai to the British Empire, as part of a British-Portuguese dowry settlement in 1665, diminished the commercial value of Bassein. In 1720, the Marathas conquered Kalyan, a port of Bassein, leading to the takeover of Thane by 1737, following which the forts of Salcette Island and Parsica, Trangipara, Saibana, Ilha das Vaccas, Manora, Sabajo, the hills of Santa Cruz and Santa Maria were also seized.

The Portuguese still held the bastions of Chaul (Revdanda), Caranja, Bandra, Versova, Bassein, Mahim, Quelme, Seridao (Sirgao), Dahanu, Asserim, Tarapur and Daman. But this was short-lived; they lost the city of Bassein in February 1739 and signed the surrender on May 16, 1739 to the Marathas. It resulted in a loss of eight cities, four major ports, twenty forts, two fortified hills, the island of Salcete (Salcette), the city of Thane, the 'Ilha das Vaccas', the island of Karanjà (Juem) and 340 villages. Following the departure of the Portuguese (May 23, 1739), the area of Bassein saw its downfall with Mumbai rising in importance by way of trade and commerce.

COMMUNITY BLOODLINES

The Portuguese officials also intermarried with the locals and their offspring were known as Mestizos (of mixed blood). The conversion of Brahmins, Prabhus, Pachkalshis, Charkalshis, Sonars (goldsmiths), Khatris, Bhandaris (toddy tappers), Kunbis (farmers), Kharpatils, Khumbars (potters), Nhavis (barbers), Mainatos (dhobis, laundrymen), Kolis (fisher folk), Mahars and Chamars (shoemakers) and Bhois to Christianity by the Portuguese brought about the amalgamation of the East Indian community into five basic cultural groups.

'Samvedi Christians' (also known as Kuparis) resided in the northern areas of Bassein, with close proximity to the Vaitarna River. Brahmin by origin, they held their lands and the river sacred. They took up professions in agriculture and retained much of their pre-Christian culture. The villagers of Nirmal, Agashi and Nandahakal were recognised by the typical red topi (cap) which they wore. Samvedi Christians have now however adapted to modern-day dress codes.

'Koli Christians' are found along the coast of Salcette, Vasai and Mumbai. They lived in small enclosed villages known as Kolivadas. Their origins are from migratory tribes who came from the Balaghat and the Mahadev hills and settled along the coast (Mahadeo Kolis, Malhar Kolis, Dhor Kolis). The Koli Christians played an important role in the building of churches and their enrichment by means of ornaments, vestments and jewels. This community is a close knit one and traditional in their values. They have a high degree of solidarity and respect for traditions and customs.

'Vadval Christians' resided in the southern part of Bassein. Their origins lay within the Pachkalshis and Somvanshi Kshatriya (warrior) class, and they took up professions in agriculture and carpentry. Like the Samvedi Christians, they do not eat beef. They are mainly from the villages of Giriz, Remedy and Sandor.

Upper-class Christians who received the benefits of an education came to be known as 'Salcette Christians'. They were mainly Prabhus, Brahmins, Khatris and Sonars who together formed one ethnic minority and were converted by the Franciscans and Jesuit missionaries between 1547 and 1600.

The other cultural group was the 'Urbanised Christians'. They were those East Indians who worked in close contact with the British and Portuguese missionaries and government offices, and had a good working knowledge of English and Portuguese. They accepted a Westernised way of life and lived in areas like Matharpakadi, Dadar, Mahim and Bandra.

Those in managerial and supervisory positions came to be known as Sutars, and there were the Bhandaris, Khumbars and Chamars who retained their identity and traditional way of life.

WAYS OF DRESS AND JEWELLERY

The traditional East Indian sari is plain and simple, comprising small checks, edged with two borders. It has no other designs on it. Young girls wear a sada or half-sari with a blouse. The colours vary from red to green with the Samvedis using a deep red. The Bhandaris wear green and the Kunbis, a dark blue. The sari is nine to ten yards long and is known as kastyache. Widows wear dark blue. One's profession also governs the length and drape of the sari and how it is worn.

Unlike the general Indian custom of using the end of the sari to drape over one's head, a large white sheet which falls to the ankles and swells up from behind is worn. This is then pinned in the front and covers the whole person. Called a vol, it is worn traditionally to church and celebrations. For other occasions there is a shorter and lighter chundhri. Although the community is culturally diverse, the dress identifies them as one.

The jewellery of the community is quite elaborate and mainly made of gold. For example:

- Dole: Chain with seven gold and seven coral beads
- Duledi: Six chains of small gold beads
- Kaputa: Large earrings
- Peroz: Three chains with large gold beads
- Shiran (large): Chain with eight gold beads interspersed with coral
- Shiran (small): Chain with five gold and five coral beads.

MATCHMAKING

The making of marriages amongst the East Indians used to be a long procedure starting with finding a suitable partner, to the marriage itself, followed by a whole range of celebrations, which are now not observed on a large scale owing to high costs and changing social mores. The whole process was complex and colourful, to say the least.

Matchmaking among the Koli and Samvedi Christians, for instance, would be initiated by the parents to find suitable partners for their sons. In the case of the Vadvals and the Salcette Christians, this responsibility was entrusted to kinsmen or godfathers, who 'explored' on behalf of the parents. On the acceptance of a favourable match, an auspicious ceremony would be performed between both parties in which sugar played an integral part. Known as dhakti sakhar, it was a preliminary gesture to the formal engagement called moti sakhar, when the boy would come of age to be married. With the Vadvals and the Salcette Christians, the ceremony was known as sakhar puda.

February and May were considered auspicious months for weddings, to avoid the period of Lent (a time of fasting) and Advent (a time of prayerful preparation before Christmas). Marriage celebrations were spread over four to five days and were often blessed on a Sunday. In the rural areas, mass weddings were a common feature during May. The bridal house would be spruced up and whitewashed in readiness for 'the' day. Diyas and fairy lights would be lit at night creating a mystical aura.

The wedding banns (official public announcement of a forthcoming marriage and seeking the registration of objections, if any) would be read out in the parish church. The bride and groom-to-be would be dressed well and taken to church by their close kin amidst great jubilation.

Preparations for the wedding would include laying in a generous supply of masalas, rice, wheat and ghee. Duck, chicken and suckling would be fattened and ceremoniously killed prior to the wedding. Invitations were mostly handed to the invitees personally by the couple. The invitation would usually be for three celebrations: for the eve of the wedding; for the day of the wedding; and for the day following. A mandap or pavilion would be erected by the villagers in the compounds of both bridal houses. The arrival of the band would set off the festivities.

Prior to the wedding day, the Samvedi Christians would perform two ceremonies: the presentation of a new sari to the bride by her relations, known as the sari-choli ceremony, and the ceremony of navalchaya vidhi in which the bride would be adorned in all her new jewellery. Several ceremonies would be observed by all the East Indian communities. The moya ceremony where the groom is shaved would take place on the eve of the wedding, following which a gold ring would be presented to the bride and groom. The guests would then present their gifts, circling a coin over the head of the bride or the groom. This ritual, known as volvani, would be performed to ward off the evil eye.

The first of the festive dinners on the eve of the wedding was the aher cha jevan at the end of which prayers would be offered for the repose of the souls of all the deceased in the family. The Kolis would enjoy an additional dinner to which only married women would be invited. This is known as gauri cha jevan. On the eve of the wedding, young unmarried girls with pots tiered on their heads and accompanied by lanterns, singing and dancing, would proceed to a well to draw water called umbracha pani. Simultaneously, they'd toss in a few flowers to appease the water fairies. This salvar ceremony is very picturesque as the girls are dressed in all their finery and carry torches, which add to the colour and gaiety.

On the morning of the wedding day, the bride and groom would bathe with the umbracha pani. On being dressed, the kanayadan or ceremony of giving away the bride would be performed with the formal blessing of the parents before the altar of the house. The groom and the bride would be accompanied to church in a noisy procession under large red umbrellas. For the wedding, the bride would wear a traditional red silk sari enriched with gold embroidery, a custom now replaced by Western bridal gowns.

After mass in church, the bridal party would proceed to the bride's house where, on entering the pavilion, they would be showered with flowers and rice. The bride's father would then gift her a gold ring and the boy's family would give her a gold necklace. A sumptuous lunch would follow. The Koli and the Samvedi Christians tend to serve an Indian vegetarian meal as they abstain from pork and beef.

Amongst urban East Indians, most of the wedding ceremonies have been done away with. After the nuptials in Church, there is a large reception with cake and wine and a buffet at a public venue. And like all other wedding customs, the newlyweds leave on their honeymoon.

ARCHITECTURAL DIFFERENCES

As varied as their cultures, East Indian houses also differed in several ways but retained much of their Indian-ness. Only the affluent built their homes in styles reminiscent of Mediterranean architecture.

East Indian villages were 'designed' on very simple principles, using materials easily available, drawing from their means of livelihood. These were set along winding roads surrounded by fields or within beautiful coconut and palm groves. Those with the means, built houses to last with thick walls and high ceilings and used Burma teak.

The Koli village houses were built close to each other, encircling the village well, where considerable daily gossip would circulate. Built on the beaches, the sea being their livelihood, Kolis tended to follow a similar pattern throughout the coastal region. Despite modern-day changes, this community has retained much of its charm.

The Salcette Christians built brick and stone houses with tiled roofs, and often had large verandas running around the house. They were built on a smaller scale, as they tended to live as nuclear families. They built close to each other and on unfertile land leaving the surrounding land free for cultivation.

In comparison, the Christians of Bassein and the Samvedi Christians built large houses using wood and had carved doors. They built to accommodate the entire family under one roof with each son sharing a separate part of the house.

FUSION FOOD

Weddings and religious feast days are the best time to savour East Indian cuisine. As in Western menus, the East Indian ones includes meats like pork, duck and beef. There are, however, members of the community in the Vasai taluka who abstain from beef and pork. Traditional East Indian cooking was done in earthenware and clay ovens. Wood fires in the rural areas along with coal, caused food to be cooked slowly and at even temperatures, which are fundamental for bringing out the best flavours.

Rice plays an important role in the diet and is mainly consumed at lunch, whereas roti and bhakri are eaten at night. The normal everyday meal is simple, consisting of a curry, a vegetable, and a pickle or condiment to go with it. Vegetables were commonly grown on patches of land adjoining homes and included white pumpkin (doodhya), yam, (suran), okra (bhindi), bitter gourd (karela), turnip (shalgam), fenugreek (methi) and several leafy greens and beans. Fruit too is popular. Mangoes, chickoos, melons, cashew nuts, papaya, love apples, custard apples, guavas, bananas and sugarcane grow plentifully in north Konkan, not forgetting that great fruit, the coconut.

Besides the cultivation of rice, which, as in all of India, centres on the monsoon, the lack or abundance of rain makes a difference to their livelihoods. The wells are often dry by May and it is a long wait till the rains arrive in June. There are two types of plantations: oonhalli (crops planted in the middle of May and watered till the rains arrive) and paushi (crops planted immediately after the rains).

The modern age has changed the experience of consuming East Indian cuisine. There is a tendency to take shortcuts sometimes, thereby altering tastes and producing results that might be below par, but which, to a stranger, are simply marvellous. It is the quality of ingredients that makes the difference in a well-cooked meal. For example, the flavour imparted by ghee (clarified butter) is far superior to that of vegetable oils. Traditionally, all masalas are hand-pounded and hand-ground, presenting a different texture from the dish for which masalas are blended in an electric mixer.

The hand-pounding of dry masalas is normally done during the hot summer months. The job is carried out by women working in pairs who move from house to house and village to village along with the heavy equipment required. Recipes for masalas vary, as families use their own proportions in spices. Hence, flavours differ from house to house and village to village. In recent decades, dry masalas in large quantities are ground in small mechanical mills in the neighbourhood. These are stored in dark glass bottles (not unusually, beer bottles) and sealed with corks tied over with muslin cloth and string.

Other essentials are stored and salted — red chillies, souring agents, such as kokum, raw mangoes, diced and soaked in brine, and tamarind, which is dried and shaped into balls for further use.

Similar to Hindu tradition, East Indian cooking rests on a few religious beliefs. The four essential elements in Indian cuisine are fire, ghee, cultivated grain and non-agricultural products. Water, milk and ghee are considered auspicious and act as purifying elements. It is taboo to compare meals cooked in ghee with those cooked in oil.

CHANGING EAST INDIANA

The blends and mixes through intermarriage have enriched the East Indians, adding to the flavours of their cuisine. Whilst links forged with Goans were strong and the phenomenon easy to understand (both communities are from the Konkan coast), other East Indian family connections were made with Anglo-Indians, South Indians and even Baghdadis. Connections down the line have tied the knot with Danes, and quite naturally in our times, with Indian Hindus from various parts of India.

Like their countrymen from other communities, the East Indians have travelled far and wide. My mother's great-grandfather, Dr Michael Fernandes, was a surgeon and was with the British in South Africa during the Boer War. His medical practice was on Bazaar Road (Bandra). The family graves in St Andrew's Church are close to the cross from old St Anne's.

Other East Indians will have equally or more colourful histories. The point is that the physical fusion must have obviously filtered into the cuisine, with a dash of Hindu coastal and a pinch of Portuguese Continental mixing into East Indian, making for slight yet subtle differences in preference.

Nana, my East Indian grandmother, for two-thirds of her life didn't do any cooking herself. After retiring from an organised career, she kept house, and relied heavily on *The Chef*, Isadore Coelho's complete guide to cookery. In it she found several East Indian recipes. Nana, having lived in different parts of India, finally settled for her remaining twenty years in an East Indian wadi in Dadar; Prabhadevi to be precise. We grew up amidst coconut trees, little cottages, a few bungalows, zopadis (huts), sand and good earth underfoot. Not far from the main road, the wadi was mostly peaceful, and serene. In the years of prohibition, everyone moonlighted, and made and drank 'illicit' liquor. There were minor skirmishes, and occasional family feuds, punctuated by Cross feasts. In most East Indian pockets in the city, a cross of stone or brick is mounted outdoors, and in May and October for instance, the community gathers around it to chant the rosary, recite a litany, followed by a feast day, with small edibles like boiled Bengal gram. Nana died in June 1981. Prabhadevi has regressed. But it is progressive too, beyond recognition!

Various Catholic communities built the Bombay Gymkhana in South Mumbai, by the purchase of land in 1914 and the gymkhana opened a year later, inaugurated by the then Governor of Bombay. However, for the East Indians it was a matter of pride to create the Bandra Gymkhana. It now stands as the gathering point for East Indian socials and functions. The gym was created as a place for youngsters to partake of healthy recreation, a place to gossip and for the elderly to reminisce. The gymkhana came about with the generous donation of a plot of land by Dr D.A. D'Monte and Mr J.R. Athaide. The foundation stone was laid in 1934, the building completed in 1935 and inaugurated on May 4, 1935 by His Excellency the Governor of Bombay accompanied by Lady Brabourne. It was blessed by the Archbishop of Bombay. Much has changed, including the gymkhana. While the affluent have left for farther shores, they have formed small associations where they celebrate Bandra Feast (post-September 8, the Nativity of the Blessed Virgin). However, and happily, East Indian cuisine is still around. Here's to it, Enjoy.

MASALAS & SPICE POWDERS

❯ East Indian Bottle Masala-1
Makes: 11 kg
Shelf life: 1 year

2 kg dried red Kashmiri chillies
2 kg dried red Resham patti chillies
500 g dried red Madras chillies
750 g coriander seeds
500 g black peppercorns
500 g cumin seeds
500 g mustard seeds / rye
500 g sesame seeds / til
500 g poppy seeds / khus-khus
750 g turmeric
500 g cinnamon
500 g cloves
500 g green cardamoms
500 g fenugreek seeds / methi
500 g fennel seeds / saunf
100 g wheat grains / gehun
100 g husked, split Bengal gram / chana dal
30 g star anise / badian
30 g mace / javitri
20 g allspice / kabab chini
2 tsp saffron
10 g bay leaves / tej patta

Dry all the ingredients thoroughly in the hot sun for 2 days; or oven-dry. Alternatively, dry-roast each spice separately over low to moderate heat in a heavy-bottomed pan for about 10 minutes each, tossing continuously, till fragrant.
Grind the spices fine with a mortar and pestle or in a grinder.
Store in airtight containers in a cool and dry place.

❯ East Indian Bottle Masala-2
Makes: 5 kg
Shelf life: 1 year

2 kg dried red Kashmiri chillies
1 kg coriander seeds
800 g turmeric
400 g cumin seeds
500 g poppy seeds / khus-khus
500 g sesame seeds / til
100 g black peppercorns
300 g mustard seeds / rye
30 g fenugreek seeds / methi
30 g caraway seeds / shahi jeera
30 g fennel seeds / saunf
15 g green cardamoms
15 g cinnamon
15 g cloves
30 g black cardamoms
50 g bay leaves / tej patta
20 g asafoetida / hing
2 nutmegs / jaiphul
10 g nagkesar / cassia buds
10 g Goa spiceberries / tirphal
10 g mace / javitri
10 g star anise / badian
10 g allspice / kabab chini
10 g sea lichen / dagadfal
100 g husked, split Bengal gram / chana dal
50 g wheat grains /gehun
10 g mugwort / mai patri

Proceed as given for bottle masala-1.

❯ Amti Masala
Makes: 100 g
Shelf life: 1 month

50 g coriander seeds
25 g cumin seeds

1 tbsp poppy seeds / khus-khus
1 tbsp fennel seeds / saunf
10 g cinnamon
15 cloves
6 black cardamoms

Proceed as given for bottle masala-1 (p. 30).

Garam Masala Powder-1
Makes: 1 kg
Shelf life: 1 month

450 g cinnamon
225 g black cardamoms
225 g cloves
25 g cumin seeds

Proceed as given for bottle masala-1 (p. 30).

Garam Masala Powder-2
Makes: 75 g
Shelf life: 1 month

20 g cinnamon
6 g black cardamoms
15 g cloves
50 g coriander seeds

Proceed as given for bottle masala-1 (p. 30).

Khuddi Masala
Makes: 350 g
Shelf life: 1 month

30 g nutmeg / jaiphul
30 g mace / javitri
60 g cinnamon
20 g green cardamoms
30 g cloves
30 g sesame seeds / til
20 g poppy seeds / khus-khus
30 g fennel seeds / saunf
20 g star anise / badian
3 g caraway seeds / shahi jeera
30 g lime seeds
30 g bay leaves / tej patta
30 g allspice / kabab chini
10 strands saffron

Grate nutmeg and mace separately.
Proceed as given for bottle masala-1 (p. 30)
for the remaining ingredients, and mix in
nutmeg and mace before storing the masala.

Aromatic Spice Mix
Makes: 150 g
Shelf life: 1 month

4 tbsp allspice powder / kabab chini
2 tbsp cinnamon powder
2 tsp nutmeg powder / jaiphul
2 tsp clove powder
1 tsp ginger powder / saunth

Mix all spices and store in airtight containers.

Curry Powder
Makes: 275 g
Shelf life: 1 month

60 g cumin powder
60 g yellow mustard powder
30 g red chilli powder
120 g coriander powder
1 heaped tsp asafoetida powder / hing
½ tsp fenugreek seed powder / methi

Mix all spices and store in airtight containers.

Vindaloo Masala
Makes: 600 g
Shelf life: 6 months

50 g turmeric powder
50 g cumin powder
500 g red Kashmiri chilli powder

Mix all spices and store in airtight containers
in a cool and dry place.

Note: For 1 kg of meat use 2 tbsp of masala
with 8 flakes of crushed garlic and 100 ml
vinegar to make a paste for the marinade.

Frithad Masala-1
Makes: 40 g for a dish of 4 servings
Shelf life: 2-3 days

15 dried red Kashmiri chillies
1 tsp cumin seeds
8 garlic flakes
1 tsp poppy seeds / khus-khus
1 tbsp coriander seeds
6 black peppercorns
6 cloves
6 green cardamoms
1" stick cinnamon
1 tsp turmeric powder

1 tsp sesame seeds / til

Remove and discard seeds of half the chillies before grinding. Cut off the chilli stalks and discard.
Dry-roast each spice separately over low to moderate heat in a heavy-bottomed pan for 10 minutes each, tossing continuously, till fragrant.
Grind all the ingredients in a blender to a smooth paste, gradually adding up to 3 tbsp of water, as required.

❯ Frithad Masala-2
Makes: 120 g for a dish of 4 servings
Shelf life: 2-3 days

Replace red Kashmiri chillies in frithad masala-1 with 100 g fresh coconut, grated

Dry-roast each spice separately over low to moderate heat in a heavy-bottomed pan for 10 minutes each, tossing continuously, till fragrant.
Grind all the ingredients in a blender to a smooth paste, gradually adding up to 3 tbsp of water, as required.

❯ Frithad Masala-3
Makes: 120 g for a dish of 4 servings
Shelf life: 2-3 days

Replace half the red Kashmiri chillies in frithad masala-1 with 100 g fresh coconut, grated

Cut off the chilli stalks and discard.
Dry-roast each spice separately over low to moderate heat in heavy-bottomed pan for 10 minutes each, tossing continuously, till fragrant.
Grind all the ingredients in a blender to a smooth paste, gradually adding up to 3 tbsp of water, as required.

❯ Frithad Masala-4
Makes: 120 g for a dish of 4 servings
Shelf life: 2-3 days

Replace red Kashmiri chillies in frithad masala-1 with:
7 green chillies
100 g grated coconut

Cut off the chilli stalks and discard.

Dry-roast each spice separately over low to moderate heat in a heavy-bottomed pan for 10 minutes each tossing continuously, till fragrant.
Grind all the ingredients in a blender to a smooth paste, gradually adding up to 3 tbsp of water, as required.

❯ Red Chutney Masala for Stuffing
Stuffing for: 1 large pomfret or 6 Bombay ducks
Shelf life: 7 days refrigerated

5 dried red Kashmiri chillies
½ tsp cumin seeds
3 garlic flakes
1 tbsp tamarind without seeds and fibre
¼ tsp salt

Cut off the chilli stalks and discard.
Grind all the ingredients in a blender to a smooth paste, gradually adding up to 2 tbsp of water, as required.

❯ Green Chutney Masala for Stuffing
Stuffing for: 1 large pomfret or 6 Bombay ducks
Shelf life: 7 days refrigerated

500 g coriander leaves
4-5 garlic flakes
½ tsp salt
100 g fresh coconut, grated
½ tsp cumin seeds
1 tbsp tamarind without seeds and fibre
¼" piece of ginger

Grind all the ingredients in a blender to a smooth paste, gradually adding up to 2 tbsp of water, as required.

❯ Basic Red Masala
For a dish of 4 servings
Shelf life: 7 days (refrigerated)

6 dried red Kashmiri chillies
1 tbsp tamarind purée (p. 34)
6-8 garlic flakes
1" piece of ginger
1 tsp cumin seeds
2 tsp poppy seeds / khus-khus
1 tsp mustard seeds / rai
1 tsp sesame seeds / til
1 tsp fenugreek seeds / methi

½ tsp turmeric powder
2 medium onions
1 tsp salt
½ tsp black pepper powder
50 g tomato purée

Grind all the ingredients in a blender to a smooth paste, gradually adding up to 50 ml of water, as required.

To cook a fish, meat or vegetable dish in red masala:
In a pan, heat 2 tbsp of oil and fry the ground masala over low heat for a few minutes before adding 500 ml of stock (pp 198-200) and 2-3 tbsp of tomato purée.
Add 500-750 g of fish, vegetable or meat and cook till tender.
Pour in 150 ml of thick coconut milk (p. 34) and simmer for a few minutes.
Serve hot, garnished with fresh coriander leaves.

❯ Basic Green Masala
For a dish of 4 servings

6 green chillies
1 tbsp lime juice
6-8 garlic flakes
1" piece of ginger
1 tsp cumin seeds
2 tsp poppy seeds / khus-khus
1 tsp mustard seeds / rai
1 tsp sesame seeds / til
1 tsp fenugreek seeds / methi
500 g fresh coriander leaves
½ tsp turmeric powder
1 medium onion
1" stick cinnamon
4 cloves
½ tsp salt
½ tsp black pepper powder

Grind all the ingredients in a blender to a smooth paste, gradually adding up to 50 ml of water, as required.
To cook a fish, meat or vegetable dish in green masala, proceed as given for red masala, but omit the tomato purée.

❯ Ginger Paste
Makes: 100 g
Shelf life: 3 days (refrigerated)

100 g ginger

Peel and chop ginger fine.
Grind the ginger in a blender to a smooth paste, gradually adding up to 2 tbsp of water, as required.

❯ Garlic Paste
Makes: 100 g
Shelf life: 3 days (refrigerated)

100 g garlic

Peel and chop the garlic fine.
Grind the garlic in a blender to a smooth paste, gradually adding up to 2 tbsp of water, as required.

❯ Green Chilli Paste
Makes: 100 g
Shelf life: 3 days (refrigerated)

100 g green chillies

Cut and discard stalks of chillies, seed them and chop fine.
Grind the chillies in a blender to a smooth paste, gradually adding up to 2 tbsp of water, as required.

❯ Red Chilli Paste
Makes: 100 g
Shelf life: 3 days (refrigerated)

100 g dried red chillies

Cut off stalks of chillies, remove and discard the seeds and break the chillies into small pieces.
Soak the chillies in hot water for 1 hour. Drain.
Grind the chillies in a blender to a smooth paste, gradually adding up to 2 tbsp of water, as required.

❯ Tamarind Purée
Makes: about 125 ml

Tamarind is to East Indian cuisine what the lemon is to Continental cuisine.

Take 50 g of tamarind and soak it in 100 ml of hot water. Mix it with a fork and let it stand for a few hours.

Press it through a sieve and keep the liquid. Discard seeds and fibres.

❯ Clarified Butter / Ghee
Makes: 450 g

500 g unsalted butter

In a heavy-bottomed pan, melt butter over low heat for about 15 minutes. Allow the milk solids to coagulate and settle to the bottom. Skim off any impurities from the top.

Remove the pan from the heat and without disturbing the sediment, pour the clarified butter into a clean dish.

❯ Yoghurt / Curd
Makes: about 750 g

750 ml milk
25 ml yoghurt culture or juice of 1 lime

In a pan, bring the milk to a boil, remove and cool till lukewarm.

Pour the warm milk into an earthenware container. Add the culture or lime juice. Stir gently, till well blended.

Cover and leave in a cool place overnight to set, and then refrigerate.

❯ Butter
Makes: about 450 g

1 litre cream
500 ml ice cold water
Salt (optional)

In a large bowl, churn the cream with a wooden spoon. When the fat begins to separate from the milk, it will form globules.

When fat has coagulated, drain off the whey. Pour cold water into the bowl and rinse the butter a couple of times. Drain off the water. Place the butter in a butter dish.

❯ Coconut Milk
Coconut is a staple ingredient in Asian and East Indian cuisines. A coconut must feel heavy and sound full of liquid when checking it. After removing the thin fibre around the shell, pierce the eyes at the top or stalk end with a sharp metal object. Drain off the water. Using a mallet, tap around the diameter of the coconut, break it open then pry out the flesh using a sharp blade or coconut scraper.

To make coconut milk, grate the flesh and steep it in about 150 ml of water, then squeeze out the milk. The first time will result in thick coconut milk. The process can be repeated a couple more times resulting in thinner milk with each dilution.

STARTERS & SOUPS

∾ Fried Aubergine

INGREDIENTS

500 g aubergine / baingan
200 g gram flour / besan
½ tsp salt
½ tsp black pepper powder
1 egg, lightly beaten
150-200 ml water
200 ml oil for deep-frying

METHOD

Slice the aubergines into rounds about ½ cm thick. Soak in water for a 1-2 hours.

Mix gram flour, salt, pepper and egg in a bowl. Gradually add the water and stir to make a batter of coating consistency. It should not be too thick.

Coat the aubergine slices with the batter.

In a kadhai or wok, heat the oil and deep-fry the aubergine slices, a few at a time over moderate heat, to a golden brown.

Remove and place on a paper-lined colander to let excess oil drain off.

∾ Fried Bombay Duck (Bombli)

Makes: 12 pieces

INGREDIENTS

12 fresh Bombay duck / bombil
½ tsp turmeric powder
1 tsp red chilli powder
1 tsp salt
1 tsp black pepper powder
3 tbsp oil
50 g semolina / rava / sooji
1 tbsp refined flour / maida

Note: Bombay duck (*Harpadontidae gelatinous*) is a soft glutinous fish found in the Arabian Sea.

METHOD

Clean the fish and cut off the heads. Wash thoroughly in cold water, drain and dry completely.

Mix masala powders with salt and pepper and apply to fish.

Heat a little oil on a tava or griddle.

Mix semolina and flour on a plate.

Coat the fish lightly in the flour mix. Place the fish in the hot oil on the griddle. Turn fish when one side is done, about 3 minutes, or till golden brown.

ᕫ Beef Croquettes

INGREDIENTS

1 egg, lightly beaten
250 g breadcrumbs
250 ml oil for shallow-frying

Filling
1 tbsp oil
1 medium onion, finely chopped
½ tsp cumin powder
½ tsp bottle masala (p. 30)
½ tsp turmeric powder
½ tsp yellow mustard powder
4 garlic flakes, finely chopped
½" piece of ginger, finely chopped
2 green chillies, finely chopped
50 g fresh coriander leaves, finely chopped
1 tsp salt
1 tsp black pepper powder
1 tsp sugar
250 g beef / lamb mince
1 tbsp tomato purée
1 tbsp brown palm vinegar
1 small loaf of bread (50 g)
3 tbsp milk

METHOD

Filling
In a pan, heat 1 tbsp of oil and sauté onion over moderate heat, till golden.

Add the spices, ginger, garlic, green chillies, coriander leaves, salt, pepper and sugar.

Give it a stir and add the mince. Cook for about 5 minutes. Add tomato purée and remove from heat.

Roughly, purée the entire cooked mixture with the vinegar.

Crumble the bread and soak in milk before mixing it into the filling.

To make the croquettes

Take large spoonfuls of filling and shape into cylinders.

Beat the egg with 1½ tbsp of water to make an egg wash.

Dip the croquettes in egg wash and then in breadcrumbs.

In a large frying pan, heat the oil and shallow-fry the croquettes in batches over moderate heat, till golden brown.

Remove and place on a paper-lined colander to let excess oil drain off.

Serve hot.

୬ Prawn Fritters

INGREDIENTS

200 g small prawns
75 ml oil for deep-frying
15 g semolina / rava / sooji

Batter
1 medium onion, finely chopped
½ tsp garlic paste
15 g refined flour / maida or rice flour
1 egg, lightly beaten
1 tsp salt
1 tsp black pepper powder
½ tsp red chilli powder

METHOD

Shell, de-vein and wash the prawns. Set aside to drain.

Whisk all the batter ingredients together in a bowl.

Add the prawns to the batter and stir to coat them completely.

Dip in semolina before frying.

In a kadhai or wok, heat the oil. Add spoonfuls of prawn mixture and deep-fry in batches to a golden brown.

Remove and place on a paper-lined colander to let excess oil drain off.

Variation: Oyster Fritters can be made in the same way.

ᘒ Balchow Cutlets

INGREDIENTS

500 g small prawns
2 tbsp brown palm vinegar
75 ml oil for shallow-frying
75 g balchow masala (p. 150)
1 kg potatoes
1 tsp salt
1 egg, lightly beaten
100 g breadcrumbs

METHOD

Shell, de-vein and wash the prawns. Soak in vinegar for a few minutes.

In a pan, heat 1 tbsp of oil and fry the balchow masala over low heat, till it becomes a rich reddish brown.

Add the prawns and vinegar and cook till the gravy thickens.

Boil the potatoes in their jackets. Peel and mash them with salt.

Divide potato into 12 portions and roll into balls. Make a cavity in the centre. Put a teaspoon of prawns inside. Cover with potato and roll into a cylinder or a round, flat cutlet.

Dip the cutlets in beaten egg and then in breadcrumbs.

In a large frying pan, heat the oil and shallow-fry the cutlets in batches over moderate heat, till golden brown.

Remove and place on a paper-lined colander to let excess oil drain off.

Serve hot.

ꙮ Potato Chops

INGREDIENTS

1 kg potatoes
½ tsp salt
¼ tsp sugar
1 egg
200 g breadcrumbs
Oil for shallow-frying

Filling

2 tbsp oil
1 onion, finely chopped
½ tsp cumin powder
1 tsp bottle masala (p. 30)
½ tsp turmeric powder
½ tsp yellow mustard powder
4 garlic flakes, finely chopped
½" piece of ginger, finely chopped
2 green chillies, finely chopped
50 g fresh coriander leaves, finely chopped
1 tbsp brown palm vinegar
1 tsp sugar
1 tbsp tomato purée
1 tsp salt
1 tsp black pepper powder
250 g beef / lamb mince

METHOD

Boil the potatoes in their jackets. Peel and mash them well. Add salt and sugar. Set aside.

Filling

In a heated pan, add oil and sauté onion over moderate heat, till golden.

Add the spices, garlic, ginger, green chillies, coriander leaves, salt, pepper, sugar and vinegar.

Give it a stir and add the mince. Cook for about 5 minutes. Add the tomato purée and remove from heat.

To make the chops

Divide potato into 12 portions and roll into balls. Make a cavity in the centre. Put a spoonful of filling inside. Cover filling with potato and shape into patties.

Beat the egg with 1½ tbsp of water to make an egg wash.

Dip the patties in egg wash and then in breadcrumbs.

In a large frying pan, heat the oil and shallow-fry the chops in batches over moderate heat for about 2 minutes on each side, till golden brown.

৶ Pan Rolls

INGREDIENTS

12-15 pancake sheets (pp. 167-168
1 egg, lightly beaten
200 g breadcrumbs
75 ml oil for shallow-frying

Filling

1 tbsp oil
1 onion, finely chopped
50 g fresh mint leaves, finely chopped
50 g fresh coriander leaves, finely chopped
2 green chillies, finely chopped
1 tsp ginger-garlic paste
½ tsp cumin powder
½ tsp bottle masala (p. 30)
½ tsp turmeric powder
½ tsp yellow mustard powder
1 tsp salt
1 tsp black pepper powder
250 g beef / mutton mince

METHOD

Filling

In a pan, heat the oil and sauté onion over moderate heat, till golden. Add the herbs, green chillies, ginger-garlic paste, spice powders, salt and pepper. Sauté till fragrant.

Add the mince and cook for about 5 minutes, till the meat is cooked.

To make the rolls

Spread the filling on the pancakes along the top.

Fold in the sides before rolling into a cylindrical shape.

Dip the rolls in beaten egg and then breadcrumbs.

In a large frying pan, heat the oil and shallow-fry the pancakes in batches over moderate heat for 2 minutes on each side.

Remove and place on a paper-lined colander to let excess oil drain off.

❧ Crumb-fried Chicken Breast/Fish

Serves: 4

INGREDIENTS

2 chicken breasts or 4" fish fillets
1 egg, lightly beaten
200 g fresh breadcrumbs
300 ml oil for frying

Marinade
½ tsp salt
½ tsp black pepper powder
½ tsp ginger paste
½ tsp garlic paste

Garnish
Fresh red / green chillies
Lime wedges
Onion rings

METHOD

Clean and wash chicken / fish and pat dry with a paper towel.

Mix marinade ingredients together in a bowl and apply on the chicken/fish. Marinate for 1 hour.

Dip the chicken / fish into beaten egg, and then roll in breadcrumbs.

In a kadhai or wok, heat the oil and deep-fry chicken / fish, till golden brown. If the breast is still uncooked, place on a baking tray, cover with foil and complete the cooking process in a hot oven.

Serve, garnished with chillies, lime wedges and onion rings.

Chicken Breasts with Sugar Cane Makes: 12-15 rolls

INGREDIENTS

450 g chicken breast
8 sugarcane skewers (see note)
250 g coal
4 tbsp oil

Marinade

¼ tsp garlic paste
1 tbsp ginger paste
1 tsp sugarcane juice
½ tsp turmeric powder
1 tsp salt
1 tsp black pepper powder

METHOD

Clean, de-bone and skin the chicken breasts. Wash and pat dry with a paper towel. Cut chicken into 8 pieces.

Mix marinade ingredients together and apply on the chicken. Keep aside for 1 hour.

Thread the chicken on to the prepared sugarcane skewers.

Grill over hot coal in a barbecue for about 10 minutes. Brush chicken with oil and turn skewers periodically.

When tender, remove and serve hot.

Note: Cut a stick of sugarcane into 6" strips. Sharpen at one end and you get a skewer.

๑ Cutlets of Sheep's Tongue

INGREDIENTS

2 cooked sheep's tongue
1 tbsp oil + extra for shallow-frying
2 medium onions, finely chopped
2-3 green chillies, roughly
chopped
6 garlic flakes, roughly chopped
1" piece of ginger, roughly
chopped
75 g fresh coriander leaves,
roughly chopped
50 g fresh mint leaves, roughly
chopped
1 tsp salt
5 black peppercorns
2 eggs, lightly beaten
300 g breadcrumbs

METHOD

Steep cooked tongue in hot water for 1 hour.

Remove, rinse in fresh water, drain well and chop the tongue, fine.

In a pan, heat 1 tsp of oil and sauté onions over moderate heat, till golden.

Add chopped tongue and the remaining ingredients, except the eggs, breadcrumbs and oil for frying, and cook for about 5 minutes.

Place cooked mixture in a blender along with the eggs and grind to a coarse paste.

Remove and shape into 8 patties. Roll in breadcrumbs.

In a frying pan, heat oil and shallow-fry the cutlets over moderate heat, till golden brown on both sides.

Remove and place on a paper-lined colander to let excess oil drain off.

೧ Meat Balls

INGREDIENTS

500 g beef / lamb mince
1 egg, lightly beaten
½ tsp cumin powder
½ tsp bottle masala (p. 30)
½ tsp turmeric powder
½ tsp mustard powder
50 g fresh coriander leaves, finely chopped
4 garlic flakes, finely chopped
½" piece of ginger, finely chopped
2 green chillies, finely chopped
1 tsp salt
1½ tsp black pepper powder
100 g refined flour /maida / breadcrumbs
100 ml oil

METHOD

In a clean bowl, mix the mince with all ingredients, except flour / breadcrumbs and oil.

Scoop out small handfuls and shape into rounds about the size of large marbles.

Roll in flour / breadcrumbs.

In a kadhai or wok, heat the oil and deep-fry the meat balls, till golden brown.

Serve hot.

Or make a basic red or green masala curry

(p. 33) and add the meat balls.

⟋ Chicken and Rice Soup

Serves: 4

INGREDIENTS

450 g chicken breast, sliced in
strips
2 large onions, quartered
4 medium tomatoes, quartered
2-3 garlic flakes, crushed
2 litres water
3 carrots, sliced in fine julienne
2 small spring onions, finely diced
25 g fresh coriander leaves,
chopped
100 g rice
3 tbsp lime juice
1 tsp salt
1½ tsp freshly ground black
pepper

Garnish
50 ml cream

METHOD

Place the chicken, onions, tomatoes, garlic and 1½ litres of water in a large pan and bring to a boil. Reduce the heat and simmer for 1 hour.

Remove the chicken. Strain the liquid and return to the pan.

Add the chicken and remaining ingredients, except cream.

Pour in 500 ml of water. Bring to a boil, reduce heat and simmer till the rice is cooked.

Taste and adjust seasoning.

Serve hot, garnished with swirls of cream.

∽ Green Pea & Coriander Soup

INGREDIENTS

200 g fresh coriander leaves
200 g shelled fresh green peas
1½ litres chicken stock (p. 200)
2 tbsp olive oil
4 garlic flakes
2 medium onions
1 tsp salt
1½ tsp freshly ground black pepper
50 ml cream

Garnish
100 ml cream

METHOD

Wash and clean the coriander leaves thoroughly.

In a large pan, cook the green peas in the stock, till tender.

Purée the green peas with half the coriander in a blender, and pass through a sieve.

In a pan, heat the oil and sauté the garlic and onions over moderate heat, till onions are translucent.

Stir in the green pea-coriander purée, salt, pepper and cream. Bring the soup just to a boil, stirring continuously.

Add the remaining coriander leaves, lower heat and simmer for about 10 minutes.

Serve hot, garnished with swirls of fresh cream.

୭ Fresh Green Pea Soup Serves: 4

INGREDIENTS

500 g shelled fresh green peas
50 g butter
3 garlic flakes
1 celery stalk, finely chopped
1 litre vegetable / chicken stock
(pp. 198-200)
1 tsp salt
1½ tsp freshly ground white
pepper
150 ml cream

Garnish
50 ml cream
4 tbsp fresh mint leaves,
shredded

METHOD

Place green peas in a pan of cold water and bring to a boil. Cook till tender. Drain and set aside.

In a pan, melt the butter and lightly sauté garlic over low to moderate heat. Add celery and boiled green peas. Cook over gentle heat for about 5 minutes.

Pour in the stock and bring to a boil. Lower heat and simmer for about 10 minutes.

Cool and liquidise in a blender.

Return purée to pan and add salt, pepper and cream.

Heat the soup, stirring continuously and taking care not to bring it to a boil.

Garnish with swirls of cream and sprinkle mint leaves on top before serving.

☙ Oxtail Soup

INGREDIENTS

750 g oxtail, cut into pieces
1½ litres beef stock (p. 199)
50 g butter
1 medium onion, finely chopped
1 celery stalk, finely chopped
6 garlic flakes, crushed
1" piece of ginger, crushed
1 tsp salt
1½ tsp freshly ground black pepper

Garnish
1 sprig of fresh parsley, finely chopped

METHOD

Pressure-cook the ox tail in stock for 1 hour after cooker reaches full pressure.

In a pan, melt the butter and lightly sauté onion and celery over low to moderate heat, till onion is translucent.

Add garlic and ginger and sauté briefly.

Add the stock and ox tail with salt and pepper and bring to a boil. Lower heat and simmer for about 1 hour.

Strain through a fine sieve and discard residue.

Serve the soup hot, garnished with parsley.

- -

☙ Caldo Verde

Serves: 4

INGREDIENTS

500 g potatoes, sliced
4 garlic flakes, sliced
150 g spring onions, sliced
1 litre chicken stock (p. 200)
200 g green cabbage, finely sliced
100 g spicy sausage, finely sliced
1 tsp salt
1½ tsp freshly ground black pepper
50 ml olive oil

METHOD

In a large pan, boil the potatoes, garlic and onions in the stock, till tender.

Liquidise the contents of the pan.

Return to pan and place it over moderate heat. Bring to a boil.

Add the cabbage and sausage and simmer for about 5 minutes. Sprinkle in salt and pepper.

Pour a teaspoonful of olive oil into each bowl of soup when serving.

Vegetarian version: Replace sausage with dried kidney beans, soaked overnight.

51

๑ Carrot Coriander Soup

Serves: 4

INGREDIENTS

50 g butter
1 medium onion, finely chopped
4 garlic flakes, finely chopped
1 celery stalk, finely chopped
1 kg carrots, chopped
2" piece of ginger, finely chopped
2 tsp coriander powder
1 litre vegetable / chicken stock
(p. 198-200)
1 tsp salt
1½ tsp freshly ground black pepper
150 ml cream

Garnish
2 tbsp chopped fresh coriander leaves
2 sprigs of fresh parsley, chopped
½ tsp mace powder / javitri

METHOD

In a pan, melt the butter and sauté onion over low to moderate heat, till translucent. Add garlic, celery and carrots and cook for about 2 minutes.

Add ginger, coriander powder, stock, salt and pepper.

Bring the soup to a boil, lower heat and simmer for 30 minutes.

Cool and liquidise the soup in a blender.

Strain into a pan and place it over low heat.

Heat through and add cream, taking care not to bring the soup to a boil.

Serve hot, garnished with coriander leaves, parsley and mace.

༄ Sopa de Lentilha com Toucinho

INGREDIENTS

250 g husked, split Bengal gram /
chana dal
75 g butter
2 onions, finely chopped
4 garlic flakes, diced
2 celery stalks, diced
3 carrots, diced
500 g tomato purée
1 litre any stock (pp 198-200)
1 tsp salt
1½ tsp freshly ground black
pepper

Garnish
200 g bacon, diced
A few sprigs of fresh parsley,
chopped

METHOD

Wash the dal and drain.

In a pan, boil the dal in 6 cups of water. Lower heat and simmer, till tender.

In a fresh pan, melt the butter and sauté onions over low to moderate heat, till translucent.

Add garlic and celery and sauté briefly.

Mix in the remaining ingredients, except the garnish. Cook for 15 minutes.

Liquidise the soup to a coarse purée in a blender.

Return to pan and heat through.

In a small frying pan, fry the bacon over very low heat in its own fat, till crisp.

Serve hot soup, garnished with fried bacon and parsley.

೦ Pato Sopa

INGREDIENTS

1 kg duck, kept whole
1 tsp salt
1½ tsp freshly ground black pepper
1 tbsp garam masala powder (p. 31)
2 tbsp ghee
1 litre chicken stock (p. 200)
200 g white radish, sliced in fine julienne
4 garlic flakes, sliced in fine julienne
1" piece of ginger, sliced in fine julienne

METHOD

Apply salt over the duck and rub in pepper, garam masala and ghee.

Place duck on a lightly greased baking tray. Bake in an oven preheated to 225ºC for 30 minutes.

Remove duck from oven. Remove the skin (use it for crackling).

Shred the duck and spread it out on the baking tray. Bake for 1 hour, basting occasionally with the drippings in the tray. When cooked, remove and place on a paper-lined colander to let excess fat drain off.

In a pan, heat the stock and add radish, garlic and ginger. Simmer for about 10 minutes.

Add the shredded duck and cook for about 10 minutes.

Serve hot.

VEGETABLES

❧ Drumstick Foogath

INGREDIENTS

500 g drumsticks
3 tbsp ghee / oil
4 garlic flakes, finely chopped
2 medium onions, sliced
1 tsp salt
1 tsp black pepper powder
2 dried red chillies

METHOD

Peel drumstick and cut into 3" pieces. Place in a pan with just enough water to cover. Place pan over high heat, bring to a boil, remove from heat and drain.

In a fresh pan heat ghee / oil and sauté garlic lightly over low to moderate heat, till fragrant.

Add onions and sauté for about 3 minutes, till golden.

Add salt, pepper and red chillies.

Fry the parboiled drumstick in the cooked onions for a few minutes.

Cover and steam-cook for 5 minutes.

- - - - - - - - - - - - - - - - - -

❧ Okra in Yoghurt

Serves: 4

INGREDIENTS

500 g okra / bhindi
200 ml yogurt
1 tsp garam masala powder (p. 31)
1 tsp red chilli powder
1 tsp salt
1 tsp black pepper powder
4 tbsp ghee / oil

Garnish
4 tbsp fresh coriander leaves, chopped

METHOD

Trim okra and cut into half, lengthwise.

In a glass bowl, whisk yogurt, spice powders, salt and pepper together.

Marinate okra in this mixture and refrigerate for about 1 hour.

In a frying pan, heat ghee / oil and shallow-fry okra over moderate heat for a few minutes, till tender and crisp.

Serve garnished with coriander leaves.

๏ Capsicum Foogath

INGREDIENTS

250 g capsicums
3 tbsp ghee / oil
1 medium onion, sliced
1 tsp salt
1 tsp black pepper powder
1 tsp lime juice

Masala
2 dried red chillies
½ tsp sesame seeds / til
6 garlic flakes, roughly chopped
1" piece of ginger, roughly chopped
½ tsp cumin seeds
1 tbsp coriander seeds
½ bunch fresh coriander leaves, roughly chopped
A pinch of saffron strands

METHOD

Grind masala ingredients to a fine consistency, gradually adding up to 50 ml of water, as required.

Cut capsicums into quarters, removing and discarding seeds and pith.

In a pan, heat ghee / oil and sauté onion over moderate heat, till golden brown.

Add ground masala and fry well for a few minutes, till fragrant. Sprinkle in some water if required, to prevent burning.

Add the capsicum. Cook for about 7 minutes, then add salt and pepper.

Sprinkle in lime juice a few minutes before removing from heat.

∾ Capsicum with Bottle Masala

Serves: 2

INGREDIENTS

250 g capsicum
3 tbsp ghee / oil
1 medium onion, finely sliced
2-4 garlic flakes, finely sliced
1 tsp bottle masala (p. 30)
1 tsp salt
1 tsp black pepper powder

METHOD

Wash and cut the capsicum into cubes, discarding pith and seeds.

In a frying pan, heat ghee / oil and sauté onion and garlic over moderate heat, till golden brown.

Mix in the bottle masala, salt and pepper.

Add capsicum and stir-fry for 5 minutes.

- -

∾ Cabbage Foogath

Serves: 4

INGREDIENTS

2 tbsp ghee / oil
1 tsp poppy seeds / khus-khus
10 garlic flakes, finely slivered
250 g cabbage, finely shredded
1 tsp salt
1 tsp black pepper powder

METHOD

In a frying pan, heat ghee / oil and add the poppy seeds. When they splutter, add garlic and sauté over low heat, till fragrant.

Add cabbage, salt and pepper. Stir-fry for about 5 minutes.

Cover pan and steam-cook for 2 minutes. Serve hot with plain or buttered rice.

❧ Moong Dal with Drumstick

Serves: 4

INGREDIENTS

250 g husked, split moong beans / moong dal
500 ml vegetable stock (p. 199)
1 medium onion, finely sliced
½ tsp turmeric powder
2 tsp salt
2 drumsticks
1 tbsp ghee
3-4 green chillies
2 sprigs curry leaves
½ tsp chopped garlic
½ tbsp lime juice

Tempering
2 tbsp ghee
¼ tsp mustard seeds / rye

Garnish
1 tbsp chopped fresh coriander leaves

METHOD

Wash the dal thoroughly and soak in water for about 10 minutes.

In a pan, put the dal with the stock. Bring to a boil over high heat, lower heat and simmer for about 10 minutes.

Cool for a while, and beat dal with a hand beater or blend in a blender.

In a pan, heat ghee for tempering. Add the mustard seeds. When they splutter, add onion and sauté, till golden brown.

Mix in turmeric, salt and dal, bring to a boil. Lower heat and simmer for about 10 minutes.

Peel drumstick and cut into 3" pieces. Place in a pan with just enough water to cover. Place pan over high heat, bring to a boil, remove from heat and drain. Add to dal.

Pour the dal into a serving dish.

In a small pan, heat 1 tbsp of ghee and fry green chillies, curry leaves and garlic for 3-4 seconds over low heat.

Pour contents of pan into dal and stir well.

Sprinkle lime juice and coriander leaves.

Serve hot with plain or buttered rice.

ᘒ Mashed Potatoes with Wild Mushrooms

Serves: 2

INGREDIENTS

1 kg potatoes, sliced
200 ml warm milk
50 ml cream
100 g butter
4 garlic flakes, crushed
2 tsp salt
1½ tsp freshly ground black pepper
3 tbsp chopped fresh parsley
20 ml lime juice
50 ml olive oil
500 g wild mushrooms

METHOD

Place potatoes in a pan of water and bring to a boil. Cook till potatoes are tender. Drain.

Mash potatoes in a pan and mix in warm milk, cream, butter, garlic, salt, pepper, parsley and lime juice.

Place pan over low heat and cook for about 15 minutes.

In a frying pan, heat oil and pan-roast the mushrooms over high heat for about 3 minutes.

Add mushrooms to the mashed potatoes and mix well.

- -

ᘒ French Bean Foogath

Serves: 4

INGREDIENTS

2 tbsp ghee / oil
1 medium onion, finely sliced
4 garlic flakes, finely sliced
2 green chillies, finely sliced
300 g French beans, finely sliced
1 tsp salt
½ tsp black pepper powder
100 g fresh coconut, grated

METHOD

In a pan, heat ghee / oil and lightly sauté onion and garlic over moderate heat, till golden brown.

Add green chillies and finally the beans. Cover and steam-cook for 10-15 minutes.

Sprinkle in salt and pepper.

Mix in coconut during the last 2 minutes of cooking.

ော Pumpkin Foogath

INGREDIENTS

250 g red pumpkin / kuddu
3 tbsp oil
2 tbsp ghee / oil
1 tsp poppy seeds / khus-khus
1 medium onion, finely chopped
3 garlic flakes, crushed
1½ tsp salt
½ tsp black pepper powder

Garnish
100 g fresh coconut, grated

METHOD

Remove the skin of the pumpkin and cut the flesh into cubes.

Rub 3 tbsp of oil on pumpkin cubes and arrange in a single layer in a roasting pan. Roast in an oven preheated to 225°C, till golden brown, tossing occasionally to brown all sides.

In a pan, heat 2 tbsp ghee / oil and fry poppy seeds till they splutter. Add onion and garlic and sauté over moderate heat, till golden brown.

Sprinkle in salt and pepper.

Add pumpkin and cook for about 10 minutes.

Garnish with coconut and serve hot.

∾ Bitter Gourd Crisp

INGREDIENTS

250 g bitter gourd / karela
300 ml brine (50 gms salt
dissolved in 250 ml water)
2 tbsp oil
1 medium onion, finely sliced
½ tsp salt
½ tsp black pepper powder

METHOD

Cut gourds lengthwise in halves, remove pith and seeds. Cut the flesh into fine julienne.

Soak gourds in brine for 1 hour and then drain off the water.

In a pan, heat the oil and sauté onion over moderate heat, till golden brown.

Toss in salt and pepper.

Add the gourds and fry for 10 minutes, till crisp.

Note: More commonly known as Chinese bitter melon, bitter gourd / karela is used widely in Asian cooking as also medicinally. The pith must be removed before using. It is quite bitter and so must be salted to draw out the bitter juices.

- - - - - - - - - - - - - - - - - - - -

∾ Ivy Gourd with Bottle Masala

INGREDIENTS

2 tbsp ghee / oil
1 medium onion, finely sliced
1 tsp bottle masala (p. 30)
250 g ivy gourd / tendli, sliced
lengthwise
1 medium tomato, finely sliced
½ tsp salt
½ tsp black pepper powder

METHOD

In a pan, heat the ghee / oil and sauté onion over moderate heat, till golden brown.

Sprinkle in bottle masala and fry for a few minutes before adding the gourd and tomato. Cook over low heat for about 10 minutes.

Toss in salt and pepper and stir for a minute.

SEAFOOD

Preferably use a separate cutting board for cleaning fish.

It's best to buy fresh oysters, clams or mussels in their shells. Cleaning them immediately before use grants a level of freshness to the finished product. Wash them thoroughly. Only clams and oysters have tightly closed shells, discard any that are open or feel very heavy. If they are heavy, it means they are filled with sand or silt. Use a heavy glove or thick towel to hold the shellfish.

Oysters: Moving a knife back and forth, pry open the oyster. The oyster should be clamped firmly on to the knife. Working carefully, slide the knife to the end to cut the adductor muscle and run the knife along the body of the oyster. Discard the top shell or remove the flesh totally and put into a bowl of water.

Clams: Follow the same principle of cleaning, as for oysters.

Mussels: Here one has to be more careful. Mussels have a dark shaggy beard to them which must be removed and discarded. Special care must be taken when cleaning mussels; those that are already opened must be discarded as they are not fresh.

De-veining prawns: The vein or black line one see along the prawn is actually its digestive track. It is this which causes stomach upsets or food poisoning. You can either keep the heads and tails on the prawns or discard the hard outer casing. Slit the back of the prawn with a sharp knife. With a toothpick or the tip of a knife, starting at the head of the prawn, remove the black line and discard. Having a bowl of water is handy for removing the vein and cleaning the knife.

Tiny shrimp are never de-veined.

Lobster: First kill the lobster by plunging it head first into a bowl of hot water. Remove and hold one end and twist the other end till the head breaks off from the tail.

Another way is by slitting the belly from the top to the bottom. Slide a knife all the way through and remove the meat pieces.

Discard the sticky membrane that comes with the meat immediately, before it dries on to the meat. Wash out the colon area of the lobster well, rinse the meat and use immediately. If refrigerated, it will keep for seventy-two hours.

Fresh crabs: Place crabs in the freezer for 1 hour. This puts them in a dormant state. Place crabs in a pan of boiling water. There should be enough water to cover them.

Sprinkle in half a cupful of salt. Cook for about 15 minutes. Transfer into a bowl of cold water before draining off the water.

Hold the base with one hand before pulling off the top. Turn it over and pull on the triangular section, remove the fins which look like a serrated fan. Throw away the intestine which runs along the back of the crab.

Discard the mushy yellow stuff — these are the crabs' organs and some people like it. Rinse the crab and break off the legs. Crack them with a cooking hammer.

Use the crab whole or dig out the meat as the recipe calls for.

∽ Dried Bombay Duck with Mango Serves: 2

INGREDIENTS

1 raw mango
10 dried Bombay duck / bombil
3 tbsp + 1 tbsp ghee / oil

Masala
7 dried red Kashmiri chillies
1 tsp sugar
1 tsp cumin seeds
8 garlic flakes, roughly chopped
½ tsp salt
1 tsp black pepper powder

METHOD

Soak the red chillies in a little warm water for about 1 hour. Drain. Remove and discard seeds.

Grind masala ingredients to a fine consistency, gradually adding up to 50 ml of water, as required.

Boil the mango till soft. Drain, remove and discard seed, and purée flesh with the skin. Mix into masala.

Wash fish and dry. Cut into 2" strips.

In a pan, heat 3 tbsp ghee / oil and fry fish over low to moderate heat. Remove fish from pan and set aside.

Add 1 tbsp of ghee / oil to pan. Add the masala and fry over low to moderate heat for 2-3 minutes, till fragrant. Sprinkle in a little water if required, to prevent burning.

Add the fish and cook for 5 minutes.

ೞ Bitter Gourd Stuffed Prawn

Serves: 4

INGREDIENTS

4 bitter gourds / karela
300 ml brine (50 gms salt dissolved in 250 ml water)
Oil for shallow-frying

Filling

400 g prawns
2 tbsp ghee / oil
1 onion, finely chopped
4 garlic flakes, finely chopped
2 green chillies, finely chopped
1 tomato, finely chopped
½ tsp salt
1 tsp black pepper powder

METHOD

Wash gourds and cut them along the top. Scoop out the insides and discard.

Soak gourds in brine for 1 hour. Drain and rub dry. Set aside.

Shell, de-vein and wash the prawns.

In a pan, heat 2 tbsp ghee / oil and sauté onion over moderate heat, till golden brown.

Add garlic and green chillies. Sauté for 2 minutes before adding the remaining filling ingredients. Fry over moderate heat, till prawns are just cooked.

Stuff gourds with filling and truss up with some string.

In a large frying pan, heat the oil for shallow-frying. Fry gourds for about 10 minutes over moderate heat, turning them around to cook all sides.

Remove the string before serving.

ဢ Stuffed Fried Fresh Bombay Duck

Serves: 4

INGREDIENTS

12 fresh Bombay duck / bombil
50 g red or green chutney masala
for stuffing (p. 32)
200 g rice flour
100 ml oil

Marinade
60 ml lime juice
½ tsp turmeric powder
½ tsp salt
½ tsp black pepper powder

Garnish
Lime wedges

METHOD

Wash, trim and cut off the heads of the fish. Slit
the fish along the belly.

Combine marinade ingredients and rub into fish.
Set aside to marinate for about 15 minutes.

Apply the masala into the belly of the fish.

Dredge fish with rice flour.

On a tava or griddle, heat oil and fry the fish in
batches, till golden brown on both sides.

Serve hot, garnished with lime wedges.

Note: The dish is usually prepared using refined flour
/ maida instead of rice flour.

❧ Pickled Prawns

INGREDIENTS

250 g prawns
100 ml yogurt, whisked smooth
50 g pickle mix (any commercial mix)
2 tbsp coriander powder
1 tsp ginger paste
1 tsp garlic paste
1 tsp garam masala powder (p. 21)
10 g dried fenugreek leaves / kasuri methi, crushed
1 tsp cumin powder
1 tsp salt
½ tsp black pepper powder

Garnish
2 limes, sliced
2 onions, sliced

METHOD

Shell, de-vein and wash prawns.

In a glass bowl, whisk yogurt with remaining ingredients, except prawns, and garnish.

Add prawns and marinate it in the yogurt mixture for a few hours.

Skewer the prawns and grill under a hot grill for 15 minutes, turning skewers occasionally and basting with remaining marinade.

Serve hot, garnished with lime and onion slices.

১ Stuffed Crab

INGREDIENTS

750 g crabs
1 tbsp oil
2 onions, finely chopped
1 tbsp bottle masala (p. 30)
4 green chillies, finely chopped
8 garlic flakes, finely chopped
1" piece of ginger, finely chopped
150 g fresh coconut, grated
1 tbsp brown palm vinegar
1 tsp salt
1 tsp black pepper powder

Garnish
4 tbsp fresh coriander leaves, chopped
Lime wedges

METHOD

Parboil crabs in water.

Remove the meat from the shell and set aside.

Boil the upper shells for a few minutes. Drain and set aside with the crabmeat.

In a pan, heat the oil. Add crab meat, and remaining ingredients, except garnish. Sauté over moderate heat, till golden brown.

Stuff crab shells with the filling.

Place crab shells in a baking tray and bake in an oven preheated to 175ºC for 10 minutes before serving.

Serve sprinkled with coriander leaves and lime wedges on the side.

෨ Curried Crab

INGREDIENTS

6 large crabs
2 tbsp oil
6 curry leaves
2 large tomatoes, finely chopped
1 tbsp bottle masala (p. 30)
½ tsp salt
100 ml fish or chicken stock
(p. 200)

Masala
1 onion, roughly chopped
250g fresh coconut, grated
1 green chilli, roughly chopped
1" piece of ginger, roughly
chopped
1 tsp chopped garlic

Garnish
6 lime wedges
4 tbsp fresh coriander leaves,
chopped

METHOD

Roast masala ingredients on a dry pan over low heat. Grind to a fine consistency, gradually adding up to 50 ml of water, as required.

Wash and clean crabs.

In a large pan, heat oil and sauté curry leaves and tomatoes over moderate heat for a few minutes, till tomatoes are soft.

Add bottle masala and crabs and cook for about 5 minutes.

Mix in ground masala, salt and stock.

Cover pan and cook for about 10 minutes.

Serve hot, garnished with lime wedges and coriander leaves.

Stuffed Bombay Duck with Tamarind

Serves: 4

INGREDIENTS

12 Bombay duck / bombil
1-2 tbsp tamarind purée (p. 34)
100 ml fish or chicken stock
(p. 200)

Masala
½ fresh coconut, grated
12-15 dried red Kashmiri chilli
1 tsp black peppercorns
½ tsp salt
1 tsp ginger paste
1 tsp garlic paste
1 tsp cumin seeds

Tempering
1 tbsp oil
½ tsp mustard seeds /rye
4 curry leaves

Garnish
1 tbsp chopped fresh coriander
leaves

METHOD

Wash, trim and cut off the heads of the Bombay duck.

Grind masala ingredients to a fine consistency, gradually adding up to 50 ml of water, as required.

In a pan, heat oil and fry mustard seeds till they splutter. Add curry leaves. When the leaves start curling, add masala and tamarind purée. Sauté over moderate heat, till fragrant, adding a little water as required, to prevent burning.

Pour in stock, bring to a boil and add the fish. Lower heat and simmer for about 10 minutes, till fish is tender.

Serve hot, garnished with coriander leaves.

Variation: Use 500 g of any firm white fish, sliced through the bone, instead of Bombay duck.

೦ಿ Kolbi Atwan

INGREDIENTS

500 g prawns
3 tbsp oil
6 garlic flakes, sliced in fine
julienne
1" piece of ginger, sliced in fine
julienne
1 large onion, finely sliced
3-4 green chillies, sliced in fine
julienne
1 tbsp bottle masala (p. 30)
250 ml fish or chicken stock
(p. 200)
1 tsp salt
50 g fresh coriander leaves,
chopped
1 tbsp tamarind purée (p. 34)

Garnish
2 tbsp chopped fresh coriander
leaves

METHOD

Shell, de-vein and wash prawns.

In a pan, heat oil and briefly sauté garlic over low to moderate heat. Add ginger, give it a stir before adding onion, green chillies and bottle masala. Sauté over moderate heat, till onions are golden brown.

Stir in prawns with stock.

Cook for about 5 minutes over moderate heat and add salt, coriander leaves and tamarind. Simmer for a minute or so and remove from heat.

Garnish with coriander leaves.

൦൦ Fenugreek and Prawn Bake

Serves: 4

INGREDIENTS

100 g fresh fenugreek leaves /
methi
400 g tiny prawns / kardi
100 g corn kernels / niblets
2 tbsp ghee / oil
1 medium onion, finely chopped
4 garlic flakes, finely chopped
2 green chillies, finely chopped
1 medium tomato, finely chopped
1 tsp salt
1 tsp black pepper powder

Sauce
30 g butter
30 g flour
150 ml fish or chicken stock (p. 200)
50 g Cheddar cheese, grated
150 ml milk
2 tbsp tomato purée
1 cup thick coconut milk (p. 34)

Garnish
2 tbsp chopped fresh coriander leaves

METHOD

Pluck fenugreek leaves and discard stems. Wash leaves in several changes of water, drain and chop fine.

Clean prawns and wash thoroughly in several changes of water.

Parboil corn, drain and set aside.

In a pan, heat ghee / oil and sauté onion over moderate heat, till golden brown. Add garlic and sauté till fragrant.

Stir in fenugreek leaves, prawns, green chillies, tomato, salt and pepper. Cook for about 3 minutes and remove from heat.

To make the sauce, melt butter in a pan and stir in flour. When it sizzles, gradually whisk in stock along with cheese. Finally, whisk in the milk.

Simmer over low heat, stirring all the while till it comes to a boil.

Remove from heat and stir in the fenugreek and prawn preparation along with the corn.

Transfer to a lightly greased baking dish.

Bake in an oven preheated to 225°C for about 25 minutes.

Variation: The fenugreek and prawn preparation may be served as a dish in itself, without baking it with the corn and sauce. Cook the fenugreek and prawns for about 10 minutes and serve hot.

⁊ Prawns with Aubergines

INGREDIENTS

250 g prawns
500 g small, round aubergines / baingan
1 tbsp oil
1 medium onion, finely chopped
4-6 garlic flakes, finely chopped
1" piece of ginger, finely chopped
3 green chillies, finely sliced
1 tsp salt
1 tsp black pepper powder

METHOD

Shell, de-vein and wash prawns. Parboil them.

Parboil aubergines. Cut in half and scoop out the insides. Reserve the shells.

In a pan, heat oil and sauté onion over moderate heat, till translucent. Add garlic, ginger and green chillies and sauté for a minute.

Add scooped aubergine flesh to the pan and sauté for 3 minutes. Add prawns, salt and pepper and remove from heat.

Spoon the mix into the aubergine shells.

Place on a greased baking tray and bake for about 20 minutes in an oven preheated to 150°-200°C.

Remove and let it stand for a few minutes, before serving.

୭ Kolbi Aksal

INGREDIENTS

500 g prawns
5 drumsticks
2 tbsp oil
1 large onion, finely sliced
4-8 garlic flakes, sliced in fine
julienne
1" piece of ginger, sliced in fine
julienne
3 green chillies, sliced in fine
julienne
100 ml thick coconut milk (p. 34)

Masala
1 tsp poppy seeds / khus-khus
1 tsp sesame seeds / til
8 black peppercorns
¼ tsp turmeric powder

METHOD

Grind masala ingredients to a fine consistency.

Shell, de-vein and wash the prawns.

Peel drumsticks, cut into 3" pieces and parboil in just enough water to cover. Drain and set aside.

In a pan, heat oil and sauté onion, garlic and ginger over moderate heat, till golden brown. Stir in green chillies and ground masala. Cook well for 3 minutes, sprinkling in a little water if required, to prevent burning.

Add prawns, drumsticks and coconut milk.

Bring to a boil, stirring all the while. Lower heat and simmer gently for about 5 minutes.

❧ Prawn Temperade

INGREDIENTS

1 kg prawns
2 tbsp ghee / oil
1 medium onion, sliced
12 garlic flakes, finely chopped
1" piece of ginger, finely chopped
6-8 green chillies, finely chopped
150 ml thick coconut milk (p. 34)
2 tbsp brown palm vinegar
1 tsp salt
1 tsp black pepper powder

Masala

2 tbsp coriander seeds
2 tbsp cumin seeds
½ tsp mustard seeds
½ tsp turmeric powder

METHOD

Shell, de-vein and wash prawns. Set aside to drain.

Grind masala ingredients to a fine consistency.

In a pan, heat oil and sauté onion over moderate heat, till golden brown. Add garlic, ginger and finally the chillies. Sauté briefly, till fragrant.

Add masala and fry till the oil separates from the masala. Sprinkle in a little water if required, to prevent burning.

Add prawns and coconut milk and simmer for 10 minutes.

During the last 5 minutes of cooking, add vinegar, salt and pepper.

๑ Kujit (Pomfret Curry)

INGREDIENTS

1 large pomfret
3 tbsp ghee / oil
3 medium onions, finely chopped
6 garlic flakes, finely chopped
1" piece of ginger, finely chopped
5-6 green chillies, finely chopped
250 ml fish stock (p. 200)
100 ml thick coconut milk (p. 34)
1 tsp salt
1 tsp black pepper powder
2 tbsp brown palm vinegar

Masala
1 tsp cumin seeds
½ tsp turmeric powder
1 tsp rice grains
2 green cardamoms
3" stick cinnamon
4 cloves

METHOD

Clean fish, wash and drain. Cut into ½" thick slices.

Grind masala ingredients to a fine consistency.

In a pan, heat ghee / oil and sauté onions over moderate heat, till golden brown. Add garlic, ginger and green chillies and fry well, till fragrant.

Add ground masala and stir till the oil separates from it. Sprinkle in a little water if required, to prevent burning.

Add stock and coconut milk, then fish, salt and pepper.

Bring to a boil, stirring all the while. Lower heat, add vinegar and simmer for 5 minutes.

ଚ Crab Khuddi

INGREDIENTS

1 kg crab
4 tbsp ghee / oil
500 ml fish or chicken stock
(p. 200)
2 tbsp brown palm vinegar
1 tsp salt
1 tsp black pepper powder

Masala
6 garlic flakes, roughly chopped
1" piece of ginger, roughly
chopped
100 g fresh coconut, grated
3 green chillies, roughly chopped
¼ tsp khuddi masala (p. 31)
2 tbsp bottle masala (p. 30)

Garnish
2 tbsp chopped fresh coriander
leaves

METHOD

Clean and wash crabs and set aside to drain.

Grind masala ingredients to a fine consistency, gradually adding up to 50 ml of water, as required.

In a pan, heat ghee / oil and fry the ground masala over low to moderate heat, till fragrant. Sprinkle in a little water if required, to prevent burning.

Add crabs. Cook for a minute before pouring in the stock.

Bring to a boil, add vinegar, salt and pepper and cook for about 10 minutes.

Serve hot, garnished with fresh coriander leaves.

∾ Fisherman Style Grilled Fish

Serves: 4-6

INGREDIENTS

1 kg fish (pomfret, surmai,
kingfish, rawas / Indian salmon)
3 tbsp oil / butter for basting
Juice of 1 lime

First marinade
1 tsp turmeric powder
1 tsp salt
1 tsp black pepper powder

Second marinade
1 tsp ginger paste
1 tsp garlic paste
1-2 tsp red chilli powder
1 tsp mango powder / amchur
1 tsp ajwain
Juice of 1 lime

Garnish
4-6 lime wedges
1 onion, sliced in rings
2 tbsp chopped fresh coriander
leaves

METHOD

Clean and wash fish and cut into ½" thick slices.
Drain thoroughly

Combine ingredients for first marinade and coat
fish. Set aside to marinate for about 15 minutes.

In a clean bowl, mix ingredients for second
marinade. Add a little water if required, to make
a thick paste.

Coat fish with this paste and marinate for 1 hour.

Grill fish over hot coal in a barbecue for 5-7
minutes. Turn pieces and baste occasionally
with oil / butter.

Squeeze lime juice over the fish.

Serve garnished with lime wedges, onion rings
and fresh coriander.

Variations:
• Use prawns or lobster in place of fish.
• Deep-fry the seafood in hot oil to a reddish brown
  colour instead of grilling it.

∾ Prawn Vindaloo

Serves: 4

INGREDIENTS

400 g prawns
200 ml water
4 tsp brown palm vinegar

Masala
6 dried red Kashmiri chillies
10 garlic flakes, roughly chopped
1" piece of ginger, roughly chopped
¼ tsp cumin seeds
¼ tsp turmeric powder
1 tsp salt
1 tsp black pepper powder
1 tbsp brown palm vinegar

METHOD

Shell, de-vein and wash prawns. Set aside to drain.

Soak the red chillies in hot water for about 1 hour. Drain and grind with remaining masala ingredients to a fine consistency, gradually adding up to 50 ml of water, as required. Transfer to a pan.

Add water to the masala, mix well and bring to a boil over moderate heat. Lower heat and simmer for about 10 minutes.

Add prawns and cook for about 5 minutes.

Mix in vinegar and simmer for about 5 minutes.

Serve hot with crusty bread.

∾ Fish Frithad

Serves: 4

INGREDIENTS

1 kg fish (pomfret, rawas / Indian salmon, surmai or kingfish)
4 tbsp ghee / oil
120 g frithad masala-4 (p. 32)
500 ml fish stock (p. 200)
½ tsp salt
½ tsp black pepper powder

METHOD

Clean and wash fish. Cut into 1" thick slices.

In a pan, heat ghee / oil and fry frithad masala over low to moderate heat, till the oil separates. Sprinkle in a little water if required, to prevent burning.

Add fish with stock, salt and pepper and simmer for about 10 minutes.

Fresh Green Pea Soup

Beef Croquettes

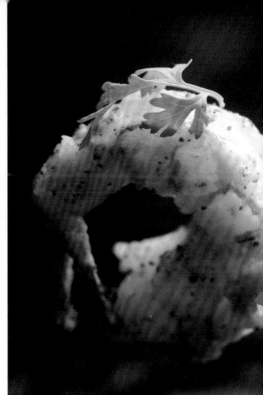

Prawn Fritters

Sopa de Lentilha com Toucinho

Chicken Breasts with Sugar Cane

Drumstick Foogath

Okra in Yoghurt

Moong Dal with Drumstick

Cabbage Foogath

Pumpkin Foogath

Prawn Green Masala Curry

Stuffed Crab

Curried Crab

Crumb-fried Fish

Fisherman Style Grilled Fish

Chinchoni Fish Curry

Baked / Grilled Pomfret

Meat Temperade

Fisherman Style Grilled Prawn

Cockle (Tisreo) Curry

Prawn Red Masala Curry

Mutton Green Curry

Mutton Chops with Bottle Masala

Mutton Lonvas

Mutton Curry

Salted Beef Tongue

Apricot Chicken

Stuffed Chicken

Chicken Curry

Duck Moilee

Pork Sarpatel

Vianda d' Alho (Pork Vindaloo)

Smoked Chicken

Appam

Fugea

Crusty Bread Rolls

Hot Cross Buns

Arroz com Coco

Arroz Pulao

Arroz de Camarao

Grilled Vindaloo of Lamb

ல Chinchoni Fish Curry

Serves: 4

INGREDIENTS

8 fish slices, ½" thick (pomfret,
surmai / kingfish)
2 tbsp oil
500 ml water
1 tsp salt
2 tsp tamarind purée (p. 34)

Masala
6-8 dried red Kashmiri chillies
100 g fresh coconut, grated
8-10 garlic flakes, roughly
chopped
1 tsp cumin seeds
½ tsp turmeric powder

METHOD

Wash fish and set aside to drain.

Soak red chillies in hot water for 1 hour. Drain and grind with remaining masala ingredients to a smooth consistency, gradually adding 3-5 tbsp of water, as required.

In a pan, heat oil and fry the ground masala over low to moderate heat for about 5 minutes. Sprinkle in a little water if required, to prevent burning.

Add fish and the remaining ingredients. Bring to a boil, lower heat and simmer for about 5 minutes.

Serve hot with steamed rice.

೧ Pomfret Bafad

INGREDIENTS

750 g pomfret
½ tsp turmeric powder
1 tsp salt
3 tbsp ghee / oil
2 tbsp brown palm vinegar
500 ml fish stock (p. 200)
100 ml thick coconut milk (p. 34)

Masala
2 medium onions, roughly chopped
2 tbsp coriander seeds
6 garlic flakes, roughly chopped
1" piece of ginger, roughly chopped
6 green chillies, roughly chopped
8 black peppercorns

METHOD

Wash fish and cut into ½" thick slices. Drain thoroughly.

Dust fish with turmeric and salt and set aside.

Grind masala ingredients to a fine consistency, gradually adding up to 50 ml of water, as required.

In a pan, heat ghee / oil and fry the ground masala over low to moderate heat, till ghee / oil separates. Sprinkle in a little water if required, to prevent burning.

Pour in vinegar and stock and mix well.

Add the fish and cook for about 15 minutes.

In the last 5 minutes, add the coconut milk and simmer over low heat.

೧ Fish Curry

INGREDIENTS

1 kg pomfret
4 tbsp ghee / oil
500 ml fish stock (p. 200) / water
1 tbsp brown palm vinegar
1 tsp salt
1 tbsp black pepper powder

Masala
8 dried red Kashmiri chillies
4 green chillies, roughly chopped
1 tsp turmeric powder
8 black peppercorns
½ tsp cumin seeds
½ tsp poppy seeds / khus-khus
½ tsp sesame seeds / til
4 cloves
1" stick cinnamon
1 tbsp coriander seeds
50 g fresh coconut, grated

METHOD

Clean and wash fish. Cut into ½" thick slices.

Grind masala ingredients to a fine consistency, gradually adding up to 50 ml of water, as required.

In a pan, heat ghee / oil and fry the ground masala over low to moderate heat, till ghee / oil separates. Sprinkle in a little water if required, to prevent burning.

Add fish, and enough stock / water to cover fish by an inch.

Bring to a boil, lower heat and simmer for about 10 minutes.

Stir in vinegar, salt and pepper and remove from heat.

Serve hot.

ɔ Baked/Grilled Pomfret

INGREDIENTS

750 g pomfret, kept whole
1 tsp salt
1 tbsp ghee / oil
1 medium onion, finely chopped
1 medium tomato, finely chopped
1 tsp black pepper powder
3½ tbsp oil for shallow-frying

Masala
5-7 dried red Kashmiri chillies
10 garlic flakes, roughly chopped
1" piece of ginger, roughly
chopped
1" stick cinnamon
5 cloves
2 tsp coriander seeds
3 green cardamoms
1 tsp cumin seeds

Garnish
1-2 limes, sliced

METHOD

Trim and clean the fish, slit the fish along the bone and cut off the centre bone with a pair of kitchen scissors.

Rub fish with salt, set aside for a while and then wash off the salt.

Grind masala ingredients to a fine consistency, gradually adding up to 5 tbsp of water, as required.

In a pan, heat 1 tbsp ghee / oil and sauté onion over moderate heat, till golden brown.

Add tomato and sauté till well blended.

Mix in ground masala and pepper and fry till the mixture is almost dry.

Stuff pomfret with the mixture.

In a large frying pan, heat 3½ tbsp of oil and fry fish over moderate heat, turning once, till cooked through.

Alternatively, place fish in a roasting pan, pour oil over it and bake in an oven preheated to 175ºC for 15 minutes, or place under a moderately hot grill, basting occasionally.

Serve garnished with lime slices.

Variation: Use red chutney masala for stuffing (p. 32) instead of the ground masala.

๑ Cockle (Tisreo) Curry

INGREDIENTS

2 cups cockles / tisreo
1 tbsp oil
2 medium onions, finely chopped
1 tsp ginger paste
1 tsp garlic paste
1 tbsp red chilli paste (p. 34)
200 ml water
1 tbsp bottle masala (p. 30)
1 green chilli, kept whole
100 ml coconut milk (p. 34)
1 tsp salt

METHOD

Wash the cockles and plunge them into hot water for 10 seconds.

Drain and discard any cockles that have not opened.

Break off the top shells of the opened cockles.

In a pan, heat oil and fry onions and ginger, garlic and red chilli pastes over low to moderate heat for 3 minutes.

Add water, bottle masala, green chilli and cockles and cook for about 5 minutes.

Pour in coconut milk and salt and simmer for about 5 minutes.

Remove and serve hot.

Variation: Dry Cockle (Tisreo) Curry: To make a dry version of this dish, omit the coconut milk and add 100 g of grated fresh coconut after the dish is cooked. Reduce the amount of water and omit the bottle masala.

Note: It is important to use only those shells which are opened as a result of cooking.

❧ Prawns with Mango

INGREDIENTS

500 g prawns
1 half-ripe mango / kairi
2 tbsp oil
2 large onions, finely sliced
200 ml rice water / kanji
1 tbsp bottle masala (p. 30)
4-6 small white onions, peeled and kept whole
3 green chillies, kept whole
100 ml thick coconut milk (p. 34)
1 tsp sugar
1 tsp salt

METHOD

Shell, de-vein and wash prawns.

Wash mango, slice and reserve the seed.

In a pan, heat oil and sauté the sliced onions over moderate heat, till light pink.

Add prawns, mango, mango seed and rice water. When it simmers, add bottle masala and remaining ingredients.

Simmer for a minute, before turning off the heat.

Note: Rice water / kanji is the water drained from rice after it is boiled.

- -

❧ Fish Amphade

INGREDIENTS

500 g any white, firm fish
4-6 tbsp ghee / oil
2 medium onions, sliced in rings
10 garlic flakes, sliced in fine julienne
½" piece of ginger, sliced in fine julienne
3 green chillies, sliced in fine julienne
1 tbsp bottle masala (p. 30)
500 ml fish stock (p. 200)
100 ml thick coconut milk (p. 34)
1 tsp salt
3 tbsp brown palm vinegar

METHOD

Wash and clean fish. Cut fish into slices or cubes.

In a pan, heat oil and sauté onions over moderate heat, till golden brown.

Add garlic, then ginger and chillies. Sauté till fragrant. Mix in bottle masala and fry it well. Sprinkle in a little water if required, to prevent burning.

Add fish and cook for about 10 minutes before pouring in the stock and coconut milk. Bring to a boil, stirring all the while. Lower heat and simmer till fish is tender. Stir in salt and vinegar and remove from heat.

Serve hot with crusty bread or steamed rice.

MEAT

Choosing Meat

The choice of meats requires care and attention.

- Buy good cuts of meat, which cook quickly.
- Avoid pressure-cooking meats as this destroys essential vitamins and does not allow the muscles in the meat to relax.
- Cuts of meat, which take long to cook, should be stewed over a period.
- Cooking time for many of the meat dishes change, according to the cut of meat being used.
- Veal and pork should always be cooked well.
- The method used to cook meats varies with the cut of meat. Two basic methods of cooking them involve dry heat and moist heat. Dry heat methods are roasting, broiling, pan-broiling. Moist heat methods include stewing, boiling and braising.
- Slow cooking for both tender and tough cuts results in juicy and tender meat.
- Cooking of meat is a compromise. Too much heat, and it gets tough and chewy. Too little heat, and it stays tough and chewy. Muscle fibre and the connective tissues comprise different types of protein and react differently to heat. As the temperature rises, the fibres shrink and expel water. The meat gets tough and dry. But at the same time, the gristles, which started out tough, get soft, the fat melts and softens the meat fibre.
- Curing meat with salt renders it more digestible, potable, and less prone to decay.
- Meat in India tends to be tough and chewy, hence raw papaya is often minced and added to tenderise meats before barbequing.

Here are certain factors to consider when buying meat:

Beef: The meat should be a bright cherry red with thin streaks of fat running through. The fat should be firm and a creamy white.

Veal: The flesh of young calves, the meat should be fine-grained and pale pink. Its flavour is less intense than that of beef.

Lamb: The meat is pinkish and the fat firm and white if the quality is right.

Mutton: The flesh of mature sheep, mutton is a darker red than lamb. In India, what is consumed is goat's meat, which is referred to as mutton.

Pork: The flesh here is pinkish white and streaked with fat, which is white and soft.

Cooking meat is an essential process, which not only enhances flavours but also kills bacteria and parasites. The method of cooking meat varies according to kind. The more tender the meat. the less connective tissue there is.

Beef is quite versatile and allows the meat to be cooked to varied degrees.

Lamb and mutton are cooked to a medium and well done stage.

Pork and veal have to be well cooked to prevent health hazards.

The use of a thermometer or a skewer is the best way of determining if the meat is done.

Ensure that the bulb of the thermometer is as close to the centre of the meat as possible.

Cooking Methods, Temperature and Timings for Meat

MEAT	STYLE	TEMP (F)	(C)	TIME / 450 g
Beef	Rare	140	60	20 min
	Medium	160	71	25 min
	Well done	170	76	35 min
Veal	Well done	170	76	35 min
Lamb	Medium	170	76	35 min
	Well done	182	83	40 min
Mutton	Medium	170	76	40 min
Pork	Well done	185	85	35 min
Cured Ham	Well done	150	65	30 min

Oven Temperatures for Roasting Meat and Poultry

	(F)	(C)	
Beef, mutton and pork	325	162	
Lamb and veal	300	162	
Roasting young birds:			
Chicken 4-5 kg	350	176	2 hrs
Duck 5-6 kg	350	176	2-3 hrs
Goose 10-12 kg	325	162	3-4 hrs
Turkey 10-13 kg	300	148	3-4 hrs
Turkey 14-17 kg	275	135	6-8 hrs

๑ Paya (Lamb Trotters)

INGREDIENTS

12 lamb trotters, cleaned
2 tbsp ghee / oil
1 tbsp bottle masala (p. 30)
750 ml mutton stock (p. 199) /
water

Masala

12 garlic flakes, roughly chopped
1" piece of ginger, roughly chopped
4 medium onions, roughly chopped
4 tsp lime juice
1" stick cinnamon
6 dried red Kashmiri chillies
1 tsp salt
1 tsp black pepper powder

METHOD

Clean and wash the trotters thoroughly. Pressure-cook the trotters in enough water to cover for 1 hour.

Grind masala ingredients to a fine consistency, gradually adding up to 50 ml of water, as required.

In a pan, heat ghee / oil and fry the ground masala and bottle masala over low to moderate heat, till fragrant. Sprinkle in a little water, if required, to prevent burning.

Add trotters and enough stock / water to cover them.

Simmer over low heat for about 1 hour, till trotters are cooked.

Best eaten with crusty bread or plain rice.

ବ Grilled Vindaloo of Lamb

INGREDIENTS

1 kg lamb chops or leg of lamb
750 ml mutton stock (p. 199)

Masala
100 ml brown palm vinegar
1 tsp salt
8 dried red Kashmiri chillies
10 garlic flakes, roughly chopped
1" piece of ginger, roughly
chopped
4 medium onions, roughly
chopped
½ tsp turmeric powder
5 black peppercorns

METHOD

Grind the masala with vinegar to a fine consistency.

Wash and trim excess fat off the meat. If using leg of lamb, cut into serving portions.

Rub masala into meat and marinate for around 30 minutes to 1 hour.

In a hot pan, add the meat and masala. Add enough stock to cover the meat.

Cook over low heat till meat is tender.

Variation: If using a leg of lamb, you can grill the whole leg over a hot charcoal fire or roast in an oven preheated to 200°C for 1 hour, basting occasionally. Serve hot.

ৰ Mutton Frithad

INGREDIENTS

1 kg mutton
4 tbsp ghee / oil
6 medium onions, finely chopped
2 large tomatoes, blanched,
peeled and finely chopped
40 g frithad masala-1 (p. 32)
2 medium potatoes, cubed
500 ml mutton stock (p. 199)
1 tbsp tamarind purée (p. 34)
1 tsp salt
1 tsp black pepper powder
1 cup fresh coconut, grated

Garnish
4 tbsp fresh coriander leaves,
chopped

METHOD

Wash meat and cut into serving portions.

In a pan, heat ghee / oil and sauté onions over moderate heat, till golden brown.

Add tomatoes and fry till well blended.

Stir in frithad masala and fry till ghee / oil separates. Sprinkle in a little water if required, to prevent burning.

Add meat and sauté over high heat to seal the pieces.

Add potatoes and stock and simmer till meat and potatoes are tender.

In the final stages of cooking, stir in tamarind purée, salt, pepper and coconut. Serve hot, garnished with coriander leaves.

๑ Sheep's Tongue, Boiled

INGREDIENTS

4 sheep's tongue, kept whole
750 ml water
2 medium onions, roughly
chopped
3 garlic flakes, roughly chopped
1" piece of ginger, roughly
chopped
6 cloves
6 black peppercorns
2" stick cinnamon
A sprig of fresh mint leaves,
roughly chopped
1 tsp salt
½ tsp black pepper powder
250 ml white wine (optional)

METHOD

Wash and clean the tongue in hot water.

Bring the water to a boil in a large pan. Add tongue along with the remaining ingredients. Boil for 1 hour.

Remove tongue from stock. Cool and refrigerate.

Cut tongue into thin slices.

Serve with potatoes and gravy.

Variation: This recipe can be used with 1½ kg of beef tongue.

﹏ Mutton Chops with Bottle Masala   Serves: 4-6

INGREDIENTS

500 g mutton chops
1 egg, lightly beaten
250 g fresh breadcrumbs
Oil for shallow-frying

Marinade
100 ml plain yoghurt, whisked
smooth
1 tbsp bottle masala (p. 30)
1 tsp salt
1 tsp black pepper powder
5 sprigs of fresh coriander leaves,
finely chopped

Garnish
1 lime, sliced
2 tbsp chopped fresh coriander
leaves

METHOD

Wash chops and drain thoroughly. Flatten lightly
with a steak hammer or mallet.

Combine marinade ingredients in a bowl. Rub
into chops and marinate for 1 hour.

Dip the chops in egg, then lightly roll in
breadcrumbs.

In a large frying pan, heat oil and shallow-fry
chops on both sides over moderate heat, till
cooked through and golden brown.

Serve garnished with lime slices and coriander
leaves.

෨ Mutton Curry

INGREDIENTS

1 kg mutton, on the bone
4 tbsp ghee / oil
Basic red masala (p. 33)
750 ml mutton stock / water
(p. 199)
2 large potatoes, cubed
1 tsp salt
1 tsp black pepper powder
1 tbsp brown palm vinegar

METHOD

Wash meat and cut into 2" cubes. Set aside to drain.

In a pan, heat ghee / oil and fry red masala over low to moderate heat, till fragrant. Sprinkle in a little water if required, to prevent burning.

Add meat and sauté over high heat to seal the pieces.

Add enough stock / water to cover meat by an inch. Simmer over moderate heat, till meat is three-quarters cooked.

Add potatoes and simmer till meat and potatoes are tender.

Stir in salt, pepper and vinegar and simmer for about 5 minutes. Remove from heat.

Serve hot with rice or chapatti.

❧ Mutton Khuddi

INGREDIENTS

1 kg mutton on the bone
2 tbsp ghee / oil
500 ml mutton stock (p. 199)
1 tsp salt
1 tsp black pepper powder
2 medium potatoes
2 tbsp brown palm vinegar

Masala
6 garlic flakes, roughly chopped
1" piece of ginger, roughly chopped
100 g fresh coconut, grated
3 green chillies, roughly chopped
½ tsp khuddi masala (p. 31)
2 tbsp bottle masala (p. 30)

Garnish
2 tbsp chopped fresh coriander leaves

METHOD

Wash mutton, cut into 2" cubes and set aside to drain.

Roast masala ingredients on a dry tava or griddle, tossing all the while, till fragrant.

Grind masala ingredients to a fine consistency, gradually adding up to 50 ml of water, as required.

In a pan, heat ghee / oil and fry the ground masala over low to moderate heat, till fragrant. Sprinkle in a little water if required, to prevent burning.

Add meat and sauté over high heat to seal the pieces.

Cook for a few minutes longer, before adding the stock.

Add salt and pepper and cook till meat is tender.

Boil potatoes separately, peel, cut into cubes and add to the curry.

Stir in vinegar before removing from heat.

Serve hot garnished with coriander leaves.

♒ Mutton Lonvas

INGREDIENTS

250 g white pumpkin / doodhi
500 g mutton, on the bone
500 ml mutton stock (p. 199)
1 tsp salt
1" piece of ginger, roughly
chopped
4 tbsp ghee / oil
8 garlic flakes, finely chopped
2 tbsp bottle masala (p. 30)
1 tsp salt
1 tsp black pepper powder
100 ml thick coconut milk (p. 34)
25 ml tamarind purée (p. 34)

METHOD

Peel pumpkin and cut into 2" cubes.

Wash meat and cut into 2" cubes.

Boil meat in stock with salt and ginger, till tender. Strain and reserve meat and stock.

In a pan, heat ghee / oil. Sauté garlic over low to moderate heat, till fragrant.

Add bottle masala and fry well. Sprinkle in a little water if required, to prevent burning.

Add pumpkin, cooked meat, salt, pepper, coconut milk and tamarind purée.

Pour in reserved stock, mix well and simmer for 10-15 minutes, till the pumpkin is cooked.

௸ Tope

INGREDIENTS

1 kg mutton, on the bone
500 g onions, finely sliced
4 tbsp ghee / oil
2 tbsp bottle masala (p. 30)
300 ml mutton stock (p. 199)
250 g parched rice / poha
Juice of 2 sour limes

Masala

2" stick cinnamon
6 green cardamoms
6 cloves
14 garlic flakes, roughly chopped
1" piece of ginger, roughly
chopped
5 green chillies, roughly chopped
100 g fresh mint leaves, roughly
chopped
50 g fresh coriander leaves,
roughly chopped
1 tsp salt
1 tsp black pepper powder

Garnish

4 tbsp fresh coriander leaves,
chopped

METHOD

Wash meat and cut into serving portions.

Grind masala ingredients to a fine consistency, gradually adding up to 50 ml of water, as required.

In a pan, heat ghee / oil and sauté onions over moderate heat, till brown.

Add ground masala and fry well, then add bottle masala. Sprinkle in a little water if required, to prevent burning.

When the ghee / oil separates, add mutton. Sauté briefly.

Add stock and cook till the meat is tender.

Sprinkle in rice, lime juice and a little more stock.

Cook for a few minutes.

Serve hot, garnished with coriander leaves.

POULTRY

๑ Apricot Chicken

INGREDIENTS

1¼ kg chicken
200 g dried apricots
100 ml brown palm vinegar
2 tbsp oil
½ cup onion paste
3 medium tomatoes, chopped
500 ml chicken stock (p. 200)

Masala
8 garlic flakes, roughly chopped
1" piece of ginger, roughly
chopped
5-6 cloves
8 dried red Kashmiri chillies
1 tsp cumin seeds
5-6 black peppercorns
1 tsp salt
1" stick cinnamon
4-5 green cardamoms
2 tbsp coriander seeds
½ tsp poppy seeds / khus-khus
A pinch of saffron strands or
turmeric powder

METHOD

Wash chicken and cut into 16 pieces.

Soak apricots in vinegar.

Grind masala ingredients to a fine consistency, gradually adding up to 100 ml of water, as required.

In a pan, heat oil and fry the onion paste over moderate heat, till brown.

Stir in the ground masala and tomatoes. Cook till the oil separates.

Add the chicken and brown well in the masala.

Pour in stock and simmer for 45 minutes or till chicken is tender.

Mix in the apricots and vinegar during the last few minutes of cooking.

Serve hot.

೨೦ Fritada de Gallinha

INGREDIENTS

1 kg chicken
4 tbsp ghee / oil
6 medium onions, finely chopped
2 large tomatoes, blanched,
peeled and finely chopped
2 medium potatoes, cubed
1 litre chicken stock (p. 200) /
water
1 tbsp tamarind purée (p. 34)
1 tsp salt
1 tsp black pepper powder

Frithad masala
15 dried red Kashmiri chillies
1 tsp cumin seeds
8 garlic flakes, roughly chopped
1 tsp poppy seeds / khus-khus
1 tbsp coriander seeds
1 tsp black peppercorns
6 cloves
1 tsp cardamom powder
1" stick cinnamon
1 tsp turmeric powder
1 tsp sesame seeds / til

Garnish
4 tbsp fresh coriander leaves,
chopped

METHOD

Wash chicken and joint it.

Grind masala ingredients to a fine consistency, gradually adding up to 100 ml of water, as required.

In a pan, heat ghee / oil and sauté onions over moderate heat, till golden brown.

Add tomatoes and fry till well blended.

Stir in frithad masala and fry till ghee / oil separates. Sprinkle in a little water if required, to prevent burning.

Add chicken and sauté over high heat to brown well.

Add potatoes and stock / water and simmer, till chicken is tender.

In the final stages of cooking, stir in tamarind purée.

Season with salt and pepper and serve garnished with coriander leaves.

๑ Frango na Pucara

INGREDIENTS

1 kg chicken, kept whole
2 tbsp + 2 tbsp butter
30 g refined flour / maida

Marinade

3-4 garlic flakes
75 ml dry white wine
1 tsp port
1 tbsp lard / pork fat
1 tbsp paprika
1 tsp red chilli powder
1 tsp salt
1 tsp black pepper powder

Stuffing

100 g ham, chopped
100 g smoked sausage, chopped
7 bacon rashers, chopped
250 g shallots / Madras onions, chopped
1 tbsp butter

METHOD

Clean and skin the chicken. Wash well.

In a large glass or porcelain bowl, crush garlic and stir in remaining marinade ingredients. Rub into chicken and set aside for 1 hour.

Combine stuffing ingredients in a bowl and stuff chicken with it. Truss (tie with thread) to seal the stuffing.

In a large pan, melt 2 tbsp of butter. Place chicken with its marinade into pan and cook over low heat, till golden brown. Turn the chicken periodically, to brown all over.

Remove chicken from pan, take off the thread and keep the chicken warm.

Strain juices and set aside.

Melt 2 tbsp of butter in a pan and stir in flour. When it sizzles, gradually whisk in strained juices. Simmer over low heat, stirring all the while till it comes to a boil. Lower heat and simmer till thick.

Serve the chicken accompanied by roast potatoes and rice, with the sauce served separately.

꧁ Smoked Chicken

INGREDIENTS

1 large chicken
2 tbsp + 1 tsp salt
½ tsp cinnamon powder
½ tsp anise powder / saunf
50 ml orange juice
50 ml soy sauce
½ tsp clove powder
50 ml olive oil

For the grill
Smoke
Coconut husk
Scented wood / cloves /
cinnamon

METHOD

Wash chicken, drain thoroughly and pat dry. Rub with 2 tbsp salt and set aside for 2-3 hours. Rinse in cold water.

Combine 1 tsp salt with remaining ingredients, except oil. Rub all over chicken and brush it with oil.

Add cinnamon and spices to the wood in a grill.

Place chicken on the grill and cover the top. Smoke chicken for 1 hour, turning occasionally. The skin will be deep reddish brown when done.

Boil or steam the chicken in water seasoned with spices of your choice, till it is tender.

Alternatively, roast in an oven preheated to 225°C, till golden brown and tender.

Slice fine and serve cold.

Variation: Duck and seafood can be smoked in the same way. Seafood needs only 15 minutes of smoking.

Note: Smoking meats or fish goes back to prehistoric times. By adding a flavouring agent and at the same time an anti-bacterial agent by way of smoke, foods were preserved over a long time. Lengthy periods of smoking dehydrate meats and fish. However, to make it here we only smoke the food to imbibe the flavours.

The meat has to undergo a further cooking process, be it steaming, grilling or boiling, to make it edible. Whatever process of cooking you use later, the food has an earthy, gamey flavour to it.

๑ Stuffed Chicken

INGREDIENTS

1½ kg chicken, kept whole
2 tbsp honey
30 g butter

Stuffing
2 tbsp oil
2 medium onions, finely chopped
2 green chillies, seeded and
chopped
5-6 garlic flakes, finely chopped
1" stick cinnamon
100 g bacon, diced
450 g bread loaf, diced
100 g shelled green peas, boiled
1 carrot, diced
200 g cooked rice
100 g seedless raisins
1 tsp salt
1 tsp black pepper powder
75 gms fresh parsley, chopped

METHOD

Wash and clean chicken thoroughly. Set aside.

In a pan, heat oil and sauté onion over moderate heat, till golden brown.

Add chillies, garlic, cinnamon and bacon and fry briefly.

Toss in bread and mix.

Add remaining stuffing ingredients and mix well.

Stuff chicken with this mixture. Truss (tie with thread) to seal the stuffing.

Place chicken on a lightly greased baking tray. Cover with a sheet of foil and bake in an oven preheated to 225ºC for 1 hour.

Remove from oven, take off the foil and brush chicken with honey and melted butter. Return chicken to oven and allow to brown.

Remove from the oven and take off the thread before serving.

๑ Country Captain

INGREDIENTS

1 kg chicken
6 tbsp ghee / oil
2 medium onions, finely sliced
1 tbsp garlic paste
1 tsp ginger paste
2 bay leaves / tej patta
500 ml chicken stock (p. 200) /
water
100 ml fresh cream
100 ml yoghurt, whisked smooth
1 tsp salt
1 tsp black pepper powder

Masala

100 g fresh coconut, grated
100 g cashew nuts
100 g pistachio nuts
7 green cardamoms
7 cloves
2" stick cinnamon
1 tsp cumin seeds
1 tsp poppy seeds / khus-khus
10 dried red Kashmiri chillies

METHOD

Grind masala ingredients to a fine consistency, gradually adding up to 100 ml of water, as required.

Wash chicken and joint it.

In a pan, heat half the ghee / oil and sauté onions over moderate heat, till brown.

Stir in garlic and ginger paste and sauté over low heat till fragrant.

Add chicken and brown it well.

In another pan, heat remaining ghee / oil and fry the ground masala over low to moderate heat, till fragrant. Sprinkle in a little water if required, to prevent burning.

Add chicken, bay leaves and stock / water. Cover pan and simmer till chicken is tender.

Whisk cream and yoghurt together, add to the curry and simmer for 2-3 minutes.

Season it with salt and pepper.

Serve hot.

Note: This dish originated with the British who enjoyed a curry made with onions and served with white rice.

ઌ Guisado de Frango

INGREDIENTS

1½ kg chicken
2 tbsp oil
500 ml chicken stock (p. 200) / water
250 ml thick coconut milk (p. 34)

Masala
10 dried red Kashmiri chillies
150 ml brown palm vinegar
2 medium onions, roughly chopped
6 garlic flakes, roughly chopped
½" piece of ginger, roughly chopped
1 tsp cumin seeds
2" stick cinnamon
5 green cardamoms
10 black peppercorns
9 cloves
1 tsp salt
1 tsp turmeric powder

Garnish
1 tbsp chopped fresh coriander leaves

METHOD

Wash chicken and joint it. Set aside to drain.

Remove the seeds from the red chillies and soak them for 10 minutes in vinegar.

Grind the masala ingredients to a fine consistency in the vinegar.

In a large pan, heat oil and lightly fry the chicken over moderate heat, till brown; or braise in an oven preheated to 225°C. Remove chicken pieces from pan and set aside.

In the same oil, fry the ground masala, till fragrant. Sprinkle in a little water if required, to prevent burning.

Add chicken and stock / water to cover it.

Bring to a boil, lower heat and simmer till chicken is tender.

Stir in coconut milk and simmer for 5 minutes.

Serve hot, garnished with coriander leaves.

౷ Chicken Curry

INGREDIENTS

1½ kg chicken
1 tbsp ghee / oil
1 medium onion, finely sliced
1 medium potato, cubed
250 g shelled green peas
100 ml thick coconut milk (p. 34)
1 tbsp tamarind purée (p. 34)
1 tsp salt

Masala
4 dried red Kashmiri chillies
2 tbsp coriander seeds
1 tsp sesame seeds / til
1" piece of turmeric or 1 tsp powder
1 tsp cumin seeds
1 tbsp poppy seeds / khus-khus
4 cloves
10 black peppercorns
1" stick cinnamon
100 g fresh coconut, grated

Garnish
3 tbsp chopped fresh coriander leaves

METHOD

Wash the chicken and cut into 16 pieces.

Grind masala ingredients to a fine consistency, gradually adding up to 75 ml of water, as required.

In a pan, heat ghee / oil and sauté the onion over moderate heat, till golden brown.

Mix in the ground masala and fry till ghee / oil separates from it. Sprinkle in a little water if required, to prevent burning.

Add chicken with enough water to cover it. Cover pan and simmer for 15 minutes.

Add potato and green peas and simmer, till the chicken and potato are tender.

Add coconut milk in the final stages of cooking, and after 5 minutes stir in tamarind purée and salt.

Serve garnished with coriander leaves.

ல Chicken Liver Pâté

Makes: 500 gm

INGREDIENTS

450 gm chicken liver
50 g butter
1 onion, finely chopped
1 tsp garlic paste
1 tsp clove powder
1 tsp coriander powder
1 tsp garam masala powder
¼tsp nutmeg powder
1 tsp yellow mustard powder
1 tsp brandy
1 tsp red chilli powder
2 tsp salt
50 g fresh coriander leaves, finely
chopped

METHOD

Wash the chicken liver abd set aside in a colander to drain.

In a pan, melt the butter over low to moderate heat and sauté the onion lightly.

Add garlic and clove and coriander powders and cook till fragrant.

Add chicken liver and garam masala, nutmeg and mustard powders. Mix well and stir in the brandy and 1 tbsp of water. Simmer over low heat for about 10 minutes.

Stir in chilli powder and salt and remove from heat.

Cool slightly and blend to make a smooth pâté.

Mix in the coriander leaves, reserving 1 tbsp for garnish.

Spoon pâté into an earthernware dish. Level the surface and garnish with reserved coriander leaves.

Chill in the refrigerator for a few hours.

☙ Duck Curry

INGREDIENTS

1 kg duck
3 tbsp ghee / oil
1 tbsp mustard seeds
500 ml chicken stock (p. 200) / water
150 ml thick coconut milk (p. 34)

Masala
6-8 dried red Kashmiri chillies
3 medium onions, roughly chopped
2 tbsp ginger-garlic paste
1 tbsp coriander powder
1 tsp cumin powder
1 tbsp garam masala powder (p. 31)
1 tsp turmeric powder
1 tsp salt
1 tsp black pepper powder
3 tbsp brown palm vinegar

Garnish
4 tbsp fresh coriander leaves, chopped

METHOD

Wash duck and cut into 8 pieces.

Grind masala ingredients to a fine consistency in the vinegar.

In a pan, heat the ghee / oil and sauté the duck over moderate heat, till brown. Remove duck from pan and set aside.

In the same pan, fry the mustard seeds till they splutter.

Add the ground masala and fry till it is a nice reddish brown and the ghee / oil separates from it. Sprinkle in a little water if required, to prevent burning.

Return duck to pan and pour in stock / water. Simmer till duck is tender.

Add coconut milk and simmer for a few minutes.

Serve hot, garnished with coriander leaves.

ᘓ Duck Moilee

INGREDIENTS

1 kg duck
4-6 tbsp ghee / oil
2 medium onions, sliced in rings
12 garlic flakes, sliced in fine julienne
1" piece of ginger, sliced in fine julienne
6 green chillies, sliced in fine julienne
2 tbsp bottle masala (p. 30)
750 ml chicken stock (p. 200)
60 ml brown palm vinegar
1 tsp salt
1 tsp black pepper powder

METHOD

Wash duck and cut into 16 pieces.

In a pan, heat oil and sauté onions over moderate heat, till golden brown.

Add garlic, then ginger and chillies and sauté till fragrant.

Mix in bottle masala and fry well, till ghee / oil separates from it. Sprinkle in a little water if required, to prevent burning.

Add duck and fry on high heat to seal the pieces. Stir for 5 minutes before adding the stock.

Bring to a boil, lower heat and allow to simmer for 1 hour.

Add vinegar, salt and pepper during the last 5 minutes of cooking.

Serve hot with crusty bread or steamed rice.

Variation: Use chicken in place of duck.

Duck Indad

INGREDIENTS

1 kg duck, kept whole
750 ml chicken stock (p. 200)
5 cloves
1" stick cinnamon
4 tbsp ghee / oil
2 medium potatoes, diced
1 tbsp sugar
1 tsp salt
1 tsp black pepper powder

Masala
4 dried red Kashmiri chillies
1 tsp cumin seeds
6 garlic flakes, roughly chopped
1" piece of ginger, roughly
chopped
2 medium onions, roughly
chopped
3 green chillies, roughly chopped
A pinch of saffron
2 tbsp brown palm vinegar

METHOD

Grind masala ingredients to a fine consistency in the vinegar.

Wash duck and parboil in stock with cloves and cinnamon for 1 hour, till most of the liquid evaporates.

Drain and reserve the stock. Pat the duck dry and cut into 16 pieces.

Heat ghee / oil in a pan and sauté the duck over moderate heat, till brown. Remove duck pieces from pan and set aside.

Add ground masala to pan and sauté till ghee / oil separates from it. Sprinkle in a little water if required, to prevent burning.

Add duck, potatoes, sugar, salt, pepper and reserved stock.

Cook till duck and potatoes are tender.

Serve hot.

ೲ Honey Roast Duck

INGREDIENTS

2 kg duck, kept whole
2 tsp salt
2 tsp pepper
2 tbsp oil
½ cup honey
¼ cup mustard sauce
(commercial)
2 tbsp soy sauce
2 tbsp Worcestershire sauce

METHOD

Wash the duck and drain well. Use the neck and giblets for some other purpose. Dry the duck well.

Sprinkle salt and pepper in the cavities of the bird. Fold neck skin and fasten to the back of the duck with skewers. Fold the wings under the back of the duck. Retain legs to the tucked position.

Grease a shallow roasting pan with oil.

Place the duck, breast side up, on a rack in the roasting pan. Cover with a piece of foil.

Roast duck in an oven preheated to 200°C for about 2 hours. Baste the duck occasionally, with the drippings in the pan.

After an hour remove and discard the foil sheet.

In small bowl, blend the honey and mustard sauce, soy sauce and Worcestershire sauce.

During the last 30 minutes of roasting, baste the bird with the honey glaze.

Continue to roast till the duck is golden brown and the meat cooked.

Remove the bird from the oven and let it stand for 15-20 minutes before carving.

Place on a large platter and serve garnished with fresh fruit.

Note: If using chicken in place of duck, the roasting time will be 20-30 minutes only.

BEEF & PORK

๑ Salted Beef Tongue

INGREDIENTS

1½ kg beef tongue
1 tbsp saltpetre

Marinade
6 garlic flakes, crushed
2 tbsp brown palm vinegar
3-4 tbsp lime juice
4 tbsp salt

METHOD

Wash the tongue and trim off any fatty globules.

Prick the tongue all over with a fork. Rub in saltpetre and set aside for 1 hour.

Combine marinade ingredients in a bowl and rub into tongue. Place tongue in a non-reactive container and refrigerate for two days.

Roll the tongue tightly and place it in a pressure-cooker container.

Place container in a pressure cooker and add water to cooker. Cook for 1 hour after cooker reaches full pressure. Open cooker when cool.

Remove tongue from cooker, cool, slice fine and serve.

ᘒ Bifes a Portugueza

INGREDIENTS

750 g tenderloin steak
3 tbsp oil
300 ml red wine
2 tbsp rum / cream

Marinade
1 tbsp bottle masala (p. 30)
2 tsp ginger paste
2 tbsp garlic paste
1 tbsp tomato purée
1 tsp salt
1 tsp black pepper powder
1 tsp yellow mustard powder

METHOD

Cut the steak into thin slices and trim off any excess fat.

Beat it gently with a steak hammer or wooden mallet.

Combine marinade ingredients in a bowl, rub into steaks and set aside to marinate for a few hours.

Smear a thin layer of oil on a hot frying pan.

Cook the steaks over high heat for 1 minute on each side. (Reserve marinade in bowl.)

Remove and complete the cooking in an oven preheated to 150ºC-175ºC for 5-10 minutes.

Add the marinade to the pan juices in the frying pan. Add wine and simmer over gentle heat, till reduced to half.

Add rum /cream and simmer for 1 minute.

Serve the steaks accompanied by mashed potatoes and rice, with the sauce served separately.

ஒ Tongue Guisad

INGREDIENTS

1½ kg cooked tongue
15-30 ml oil, if required
2 tbsp ghee / oil
2 medium onions, finely sliced
2 green chillies, finely sliced
100 g cooked mince (beef / mutton)
1 tsp salt
1 tsp black pepper powder

Masala
6-12 dried red chillies
2 tbsp coriander seeds
1 tsp cumin seeds
8 black peppercorns
10 garlic flakes, roughly chopped
2 tsp sesame seeds / til
½ tsp turmeric powder
6 cloves
6 green cardamoms
1" stick cinnamon
2 tsp poppy seeds / khus-khus

Garnish
2 eggs, hard-boiled and sliced
1-2 sprigs fresh coriander leaves, chopped

METHOD

Heat the oven to 200°C. Place the cooked tongue in a baking tray and brush 50 ml of water over it. Braise it in the oven, till golden brown. Or lightly brown it in a hot pan with 15-30 ml of oil.

Cut the tongue into 2" cubes.

Grind masala ingredients to a fine consistency, gradually adding up to 100 ml of water, as required.

In a pan, heat 2 tbsp ghee / oil and sauté onions over moderate heat, till brown.

Add green chillies to the pan, then the ground masala.

Fry for 5 minutes, stirring frequently, till fragrant. Sprinkle in a little water if required, to prevent burning.

Add the tongue and the mince and simmer for 10 minutes.

Stir in salt and pepper.

Serve garnished with hard-boiled eggs and coriander leaves.

௸ Beef Mince

INGREDIENTS

3 medium potatoes, diced
200 g shelled green peas
2 tbsp oil
2 medium onions, finely diced
3 tbsp vindaloo masala (p. 31)
750 g beef mince
2 tbsp brown palm vinegar
1 tsp sugar
50 ml beef stock (p. 199)
1 tsp salt
1 tsp black pepper powder

Garnish
100 g fresh coriander leaves,
chopped

METHOD

Boil the potatoes and green peas in water till tender. Drain and set aside.

In a pan, heat the oil and sauté the onions over moderate heat, till golden brown.

Add vindaloo masala and fry till fragrant. Sprinkle in a little water if required, to prevent burning.

Add the mince, cooked vegetables, vinegar and sugar. Stir for a few minutes, add stock / water and cook for 10 minutes.

Season with salt and pepper and serve hot garnished with coriander leaves.

ஓ Beef Crumb Chops

INGREDIENTS

750 g beef sirloin / undercut
1 egg
1 tbsp milk
1 tsp salt
1½ tsp black pepper powder
250 g fresh breadcrumbs
Oil for shallow-frying

Marinade

1 tsp ginger paste
1 tsp garlic paste
50 ml rum
1 tsp yellow mustard powder
2 tbsp tomato paste
1 tsp soy sauce

Garnish

2 medium onions, sliced in rings
3 limes, cut into wedges

METHOD

Wash and trim excess fat off the meat. Cut into thin slices.

Place the meat between sheets of butter paper or cloth.

Using a steak hammer or wooden mallet, beat it flat taking care not to tear the meat.

In a clean bowl, whisk ginger and garlic paste before adding the remaining marinade ingredients.

Add the meat and allow to marinate for 1 hour.

Whisk egg and milk together in a small bowl, along with salt and pepper.

Dip meat slices in egg, then lightly roll in breadcrumbs.

In a non-stick, shallow frying pan, heat a little oil and shallow-fry the chops on both sides, till golden brown.

Heat a little oil in a small pan and sauté onion rings till soft.

Serve chops garnished with sautéed onion rings and lime wedges.

ଡ଼ Meat Ball Curry

INGREDIENTS

Meat balls made with 500 g beef mince (p. 45)

Masala
6 green chillies, roughly chopped
1 tbsp lime juice
6-8 garlic flakes, roughly chopped
1" piece of ginger, roughly chopped
200 gm fresh coriander leaves, roughly chopped
1 medium onion, roughly chopped
1 tsp cumin seeds
2 tsp poppy seeds / khus-khus
1 tsp mustard seeds
1 tsp sesame seeds / til
1 tsp fenugreek / methi seeds
½ tsp turmeric powder
1" stick cinnamon
4 cloves
½ tsp salt
½ tsp black pepper powder

Gravy
2 tbsp oil
500 ml beef stock (p. 199)
150 ml thick coconut milk (p. 34)

Garnish
200 g chopped fresh coriander leaves

METHOD

Grind masala ingredients to a fine consistency, gradually adding up to 100 ml of water, as required.

In a pan, heat 2 tbsp of oil and fry the ground masala for about 5 minutes, stirring frequently. Sprinkle in a little water if required, to prevent burning.

Pour in the stock and stir till well blended.

Add the meatballs and cook gently for about 10 minutes.

Pour in coconut milk and simmer for another 10 minutes.

Serve hot, garnished with coriander leaves.

Variation: This recipe works for lamb mince as well. In this case, use mutton stock,

൭ Meat Curry Temparade

INGREDIENTS

1 kg beef
4 tbsp ghee / oil
1 medium onion, finely sliced
500 ml beef stock (p. 199)
75 g fresh coconut, ground

Masala
2 tbsp coriander seeds
4 green chillies, roughly chopped
6 garlic flakes, roughly chopped
1" piece of ginger, roughly chopped
½ tsp black peppercorns
½ tsp turmeric powder
1 tsp cumin seeds
1 tsp salt

Garnish
4 tbsp fresh coriander leaves, chopped

METHOD

Wash the meat and cut into 2" cubes.

Grind masala ingredients to a fine consistency, gradually adding up to 100 ml of water, as required.

In a pan, heat ghee / oil and sauté the onion over moderate heat, till golden brown.

Add the ground masala and sauté till the oil separates. Sprinkle in a little water if required, to prevent burning.

Add meat with stock and cook till meat is tender.

Stir in coconut during the final stages of cooking.

Serve hot garnished with coriander leaves.

Variation: Pre-boiled potatoes and other vegetables may be added to the pan at the end.

൜ Beef with Fenugreek

INGREDIENTS

3 medium potatoes, diced
200 g shelled green peas
1 tbsp oil / ghee
2 medium onions, finely diced
1 tbsp bottle masala (p. 30)
750 g beef mince
50 g fenugreek / methi leaves, finely
chopped
1 tsp salt
1 tsp black pepper powder
100 ml beef stock (p. 199) / water

Garnish
4 tbsp fresh coriander leaves,
chopped

METHOD

Boil the potatoes and green peas in water till
tender. Drain and set aside.

In a pan, heat the oil and sauté the onions lightly
over moderate heat.

Stir in the bottle masala and sauté briefly.

Add mince, cooked vegetables, fenugreek
leaves, salt and pepper. Fry for a few minutes.

Pour in stock / water, bring to a boil, lower heat
and simmer for 5 minutes.

Serve hot garnished with coriander leaves.

- - - - - - - - - - - - - - - - - - -

൜ Feijodia

INGREDIENTS

250 g dried kidney beans
1 tsp oil
2 medium onions, finely diced
150 g sausage mix (p. 120)
2 medium potatoes, diced and
parboiled
2 medium tomatoes, blanched,
peeled and finely chopped
500 ml beef stock (p. 199)

Garnish
200 g chopped fresh coriander leaves

METHOD

Wash beans and soak overnight in water.

In a pan, heat the oil and lightly sauté the onions
over moderate heat, till golden brown.

Add the sausage mix, beans and potatoes.

Stir for 2 minutes before adding the tomatoes.

Cook for about 30 minutes.

Serve hot with crusty bread.

৬৮ Chourice

INGREDIENTS

1 kg pork
250 g salt
500 ml brown palm vinegar

Masala-1
1 whole head garlic, roughly chopped
1-2 tbsp bottle masala (p. 30)
½ tsp turmeric powder
1 tsp cinnamon powder
500 ml brown palm vinegar
2 tbsp salt
OR
Masala-2
6 green cardamoms, crushed
6-8 cloves
8 black peppercorns
1 tsp cumin seeds
10-12 flakes garlic, roughly chopped
15 dried red Kashmiri chillies
1 tsp turmeric powder
1" stick cinnamon
2 tbsp salt

METHOD

Wash meat and dice it. Mix in the salt and set aside for 2-3 hours.

Squeeze the meat pieces in your hands, to extract all moisture.

Grind either masala ingredients to a fine consistency with the vinegar.

Add the drained meat to the vinegar mixture.

Store in a sterilised glass jar for up to 2 weeks. Use as desired or stuff into sausage casing.

ೲ Pork Sarpatel

INGREDIENTS

250 g pork liver
1 kg pork
1 tbsp + 3 tbsp ghee / oil
2 tbsp bottle masala (p. 30)
15 garlic flakes, finely chopped
2" piece of ginger, finely chopped
6 green chillies, seeded and
sliced
750 ml beef stock (p. 199)
1 tsp salt
100 ml brown palm vinegar

METHOD

Wash the liver and meat and dice fine.

In a pan, heat 1 tbsp ghee / oil and fry the liver over moderate heat, till brown. Remove liver from pan and transfer to a bowl.

Add meat to pan and fry, till brown. Transfer to bowl containing liver.

Sprinkle liver and meat with bottle masala and mix well. Set aside.

In a fresh pan, heat 3 tbsp ghee / oil and fry the garlic and ginger till fragrant. Add the chillies and sauté briefly.

Add the liver and meat, stir well and pour in the stock. Bring to a boil, lower heat and simmer for 15 minutes before adding the salt and vinegar.

Simmer for 1 hour till liver and meat are tender.

Serve with crusty bread or rice.

Note: The East Indian sarpatel is different from its Goan cousin in that it uses dry bottle masala. The Goans use freshly ground spices.

๑ Vianda d' Alho

INGREDIENTS

1 kg pork
100 ml + 1 tbsp brown palm vinegar
4 tbsp ghee / oil
1 tsp salt
1 tsp black pepper powder
750 ml chicken stock (p. 200) / water

Masala
15 dried red Kashmiri chillies
1 whole head garlic, roughly chopped
3 tbsp cumin seeds
1 tsp turmeric powder
1" piece of ginger, roughly chopped
A pinch of saffron strands

METHOD

Wash meat and cut into large cubes. Trim off excess fat, leaving a few pieces for flavour.

Grind masala ingredients to a fine consistency in 100 ml vinegar.

Rub ground masala into meat and set aside to marinate overnight.

In a deep pan, heat ghee / oil and sauté the meat with some of the fat pieces.

Add the marinade liquid and stock / water and simmer over low to moderate heat for about 1 hour, till the meat is tender.

Stir in salt, pepper and 1 tbsp of vinegar during the last 5 minutes of cooking.

Serve hot with crusty bread or rice.

∾ Pork Baffad

INGREDIENTS

1 kg pork
2 tbsp sea salt
2 tbsp oil
2 onions, finely sliced
1 tsp salt
1 tsp pepper
2 tbsp brown palm vinegar

Masala
6-8 dried Kashmiri chillies
1 tsp cumin seeds
8 black peppercorns
A pinch of saffron strands
12 garlic flakes, roughly chopped
1" piece of ginger, roughly
chopped

METHOD

Wash the meat, pat dry and cut into 1" cubes

Rub salt into the meat and set aside to marinate for 1 hour. Rinse the meat to remove excess salt.

Grind masala ingredients to a fine consistency, gradually adding up to 100 ml of water, as required.

Mix the ground masala into the meat and set aside to marinate for 1 hour.

In a pan, heat the oil and sauté the onions over moderate heat, till brown.

Add the meat and marinade and stir-fry for a few minutes. Pour in 200 ml of water and simmer, till meat is tender.

Stir in the salt, pepper and vinegar during the last 10 minutes of cooking.

Serve hot.

ഌ Pork Alimore

INGREDIENTS

1 kg pork
3 medium potatoes, finely diced
3 medium carrots, finely diced
200 g shelled green peas
1 tbsp ghee / oil
12 garlic flakes, sliced in fine
julienne
1" piece of ginger, sliced in fine
julienne
2 medium onions, finely diced
4 green chillies, sliced in fine
julienne
2 tsp garam masala powder (p. 31)
1 tsp salt
1 tsp black pepper powder
200 ml chicken stock (p. 200) /
water
2-3 tbsp brown palm vinegar

Garnish
4 tbsp fresh coriander leaves,
chopped

METHOD

Wash the meat and cut into large pieces.

Boil potatoes, carrots and green peas separately, till tender. Drain and set aside.

In a pan, heat ghee / oil and fry the garlic and ginger over low to moderate heat, till fragrant.

Add onions, chillies, garam masala, salt and pepper. Cook the masala well, till fragrant. Sprinkle in a little water if required, to prevent burning.

Add the meat and sauté over high heat to seal the pieces.

Stir in stock / water and vinegar.

Simmer over moderate heat, till the meat is almost cooked. Add the vegetables and cook, till meat is tender.

Serve hot garnished with coriander leaves.

Variation: This recipe works for mutton as well. In this case use mutton stock.

ಲ Pork Tamriad

INGREDIENTS

1 kg pork
4 tbsp ghee / oil
4 medium onions, sliced in fine
julienne
4 garlic flakes, sliced in fine julienne
1" piece of ginger, sliced in fine
julienne
3 green chillies, sliced in fine
julienne
750 ml chicken stock (p. 200) /
water
1 tsp salt
1 tsp black pepper powder
1 tbsp brown palm vinegar

Masala
8 dried red Kashmiri chillies
1 tsp cumin seeds
½ tsp turmeric powder
10 garlic flakes, roughly chopped
1" stick cinnamon
6 cloves

METHOD

Wash the meat and cut into 2" cubes.

Grind masala ingredients to a fine consistency, gradually adding up to 100 ml of water, as required.

In a large pan, heat ghee / oil and sauté onions, garlic, ginger and chillies, till onions are golden brown.

Add the ground masala and fry it well. Sprinkle in a little water if required, to prevent burning.

Add meat and sauté over high heat to seal the pieces.

Pour in stock / water, lower heat and simmer for 1 hour.

Stir in salt, pepper and vinegar during the last 5 minutes of cooking.

Serve hot.

๛ Suckling Pig with Stuffing

INGREDIENTS

1 suckling pig
300 ml brine (50 gms salt
dissolved in 250 ml water)
2 tbsp garlic paste
1 tbsp ginger paste
2 tbsp lime juice
1 tbsp salt
3 tbsp oil
150 ml honey for basting

Masala

1 tsp turmeric powder
1 tsp cumin seeds
10 cloves
1" stick cinnamon
1 tsp black peppercorns
2 tbsp brown palm vinegar

METHOD

To prepare the suckling

Wash the suckling and marinate in brine for a few hours.

Grind masala ingredients to a fine consistency with the vinegar.

Rinse suckling well, pat dry and rub in ground masala. Set aside for about 2-3 hours.

Stuffing

In a pan, heat the oil and sauté the onions over moderate heat, till golden brown,

Add green chillies, garlic, cinnamon, bacon and bread. Sauté briefly.

Mix in remaining stuffing ingredients.

To complete the dish

Fill the suckling with the stuffing.

Prick the skin with a trussing needle or skewer in several places.

Place the suckling on to a large greased baking tray.

Roast in an oven preheated to 200ºC-225ºC for about 2 hours. Baste with honey and pan juices occasionally.

Check the doneness of the meat by piercing it with a needle or skewer. If it goes in easily, the meat is cooked.

Stuffing

1 tbsp oil
2 medium onions, finely chopped
2 green chillies, seeded and finely chopped
5-6 garlic flakes, finely chopped
1" stick cinnamon
100 g bacon, diced
450 g bread loaf, diced
100 g shelled green peas, boiled
2 medium carrots, chopped
500 g cooked rice
100 g almonds, blanched, peeled and kept whole
50 g fresh parsley, finely chopped
100 g seedless raisins
½ tsp salt
½ tsp black pepper powder

Garnish
2 apples, sliced
10 lime wedges
10 tomato wedges

When the outside is a nice golden brown, remove and place on to a large tray. (If the suckling has turned brown and the meat is not tender, cover it with a sheet of foil and continue cooking.)

Garnish the tray with apples, lemon wedges and tomatoes.

Note: The suckling needs to be roasted for about 25 minutes per 500 g of meat. The weight of a suckling can vary from 2½-5 kg.

๑ Porco a' Alentejana

INGREDIENTS

750 g pork tenderloin, kept whole
750 g clams
3 tbsp olive oil
1 onion, finely chopped
3 flakes garlic, crushed
50 g fresh parsley, finely chopped
1 tbsp tomato purée
1 tsp red chilli powder

Marinade
350 ml white wine
3 flakes garlic, crushed
1 tsp salt
1 tsp black pepper powder

Garnish
4 tbsp fresh coriander leaves,
chopped

METHOD

Wash the tenderloin and pat dry.

In a glass or porcelain bowl, combine marinade ingredients. Rub into meat and set aside to marinate for a few hours.

Wash clams and plunge them into hot water for 10 seconds.

Drain and discard any clams that have not opened.

Prise the flesh off the shells and pat dry.

In a large frying pan that can hold the tenderloin, heat oil and sauté onion over moderate heat, till translucent.

Add garlic and parsley and give it a stir.

Add the tenderloin and brown it evenly.

Stir in tomato purée, chilli powder and leftover marinade and simmer for 1 hour.

Add clams and stir for 3 minutes.

Slice the meat and arrange in a serving platter. Spoon the clams and sauce around the meat.

BREADS

While making the dough for breads, the quantity of liquid that is added varies according to the gluten content and strength of the flour. So start mixing the flour with a little liquid to begin with, adding more as you go along, till you achieve the right consistency for the dough.

๛ Appam

INGREDIENTS

250 g rice
10 g yeast
2 tbsp sugar
80 ml thick coconut milk (p. 34)
1 tbsp oil

METHOD

Wash the rice and soak in water for 3 hours. Drain and grind fine.

Pass through a sieve and discard the residue. Grind the sieved rice again.

Dissolve the yeast and sugar in 50 ml of water. Set aside for 10 minutes to froth up.

Mix the yeast into the ground rice and set aside to rise for at least 15 minutes.

Stir in coconut milk. Gradually add 500 ml of water to make a thin batter. Set aside for 4 hours.

Ladle a spoonful of batter into a hot and greased, thick-bottomed, flat dosai pan. Holding the edges of the pan, swirl the batter around to give the edges a lacy effect.

Cover pan and cook for 30 seconds.

Remove and serve hot with a gravy dish.

Note: This dish, though from south India, makes for an excellent combination with the spiciness of a hot vindaloo.

৶ Apa de Aroz

INGREDIENTS

250 ml water
½ tsp salt
500 g rice flour
150 ml thick coconut milk (p. 34)

METHOD

Boil the water and stir in salt and flour.

Leaving a wooden spoon in the centre, cover the pan. (The spoon prevents the mix from coagulating in the centre.)

Place the pan on a hot tava over low heat and cook the dough for 2-3 minutes. Do not stir it. It should have a sludge-like consistency.

When the dough is cool enough to handle, knead it on a marble surface, till smooth, adding water or flour if required. The end result should be a soft and pliable dough.

Moisten your hands and divide the dough into 12 portions. Shape into balls and press lightly on a smooth surface to make a 6" disc.

Heat a tava and bake each apa on both sides till it puffs up.

ॐ Oria

Makes: 12 oria

INGREDIENTS

15 g yeast
10 g + 100 g sugar
250 g rice flour
250 g refined flour / maida
250 g husked, split black gram
flour / urad dal
A pinch of salt
450 ml oil

METHOD

Dissolve yeast and 10 g sugar in 50 ml of warm water. Set aside for 10 minutes for the yeast to froth up.

In a bowl, mix all the ingredients, except the oil. Set aside overnight.

Mix well and divide the dough into 12 portions. Shape into doughnuts.

In a wok, heat the oil and deep-fry the orias over moderate heat, till golden brown.

Remove and place on a paper-lined colander to let excess oil drain off.

Serve at breakfast with condiments and coconut chutney.

Note: Depending on the gluten content, the strength of flour varies. So you may need a little more moisture to get the right consistency in the dough.

Variation: Use 200 ml of toddy in place of yeast and water.

৯৩ Chittap

INGREDIENTS

500 g rice flour
250 g whole wheat flour / atta
15 g yeast
100 g sugar
1 egg, lightly beaten
200 ml thick coconut milk (p. 34)
1 tbsp oil

METHOD

Sift the flours together into a bowl.

Dissolve the yeast and sugar in 250 ml of warm water and whisk it into the flour with the egg to make a thick batter. Add more water if required.

Let the batter ferment for a few hours or overnight in the refrigerator.

Add the coconut milk and stir the batter well.

In a hot non-stick frying pan, smear a little oil. Add a ladle of batter and spread it in the pan.

Place a lid on the pan and cook it for 1 minute.

Serve hot with gravy or fried fish.

Note: Depending on the gluten content, the strength of flour varies. So you may need a little more moisture to get the right consistency in the dough.

ೞ Fugea 1

INGREDIENTS

250 g husked, split black gram
flour / urad dal
250 g rice flour
250 g refined flour / maida
2 eggs, lightly beaten
10 g yeast + 300 ml water or 300
ml toddy
1 tbsp sugar
450 ml ghee / oil

METHOD

Sift the flours into a bowl.

Mix the flour well with the remaining ingredients,
except ghee / oil. Leave the dough overnight to
rise if using toddy, or mix it with yeast and let it
stand for 1-2 hours.

Knead the dough again.

Take a handful of dough and squeezing it
between the thumb and forefinger, pluck out
marble-sized balls with the other hand.

In a wok, heat ghee / oil and fry fugeas over low
to moderate heat, in batches if necessary, till
golden brown.

Remove and place on a paper-lined colander to
let excess oil drain off.

ೞ Fugea 2

Makes: 24 Fugea

INGREDIENTS

500 g refined flour / maida
A pinch of salt
100 g paneer, grated
2 eggs, lightly beaten
10 g yeast + 300 ml water or
300 ml toddy
15 g sugar
100 ml thick coconut milk (p. 34)
450 ml ghee / oil

METHOD

Prepare and fry the Fugea as given for Fugea 1

136

৯ Pao de Quijo

INGREDIENTS

500 g tapioca flour
2 eggs, lightly beaten
A pinch of salt
150 g goat's cheese, grated
125 g butter
75 ml milk
1 tbsp margarine for greasing

METHOD

In a bowl, combine flour, eggs, salt and cheese and knead to make a soft dough.

Incorporate the butter and knead in the milk slowly.

Divide dough into 12 portions and shape into 2" balls.

Place pao on a baking tray lightly greased with margarine.

Set aside for 1 hour.

Bake in an oven preheated to 225°C for about 30 minutes, till golden brown.

Transfer to a wire rack to cool.

∾ Dinner Rolls

INGREDIENTS

500 g refined flour / maida
300 ml water
30 g sugar
30 g yeast
30 g butter
1 tsp salt
1 tbsp margarine for greasing
1 egg, lightly beaten
1 tsp oil

Flavouring and Topping
(optional)
Poppy seeds

METHOD

Sift the flour into a bowl.

Mix water, sugar and yeast to a smooth paste. Set aside for 10 minutes for the yeast to froth up.

Make a well in the flour and add the yeast. Mix and knead to make a smooth dough.

Transfer dough to a clean bowl lightly dusted with flour and cover bowl with cling wrap. Set aside to rise to double its volume.

Knead dough again. Rub in butter and salt and knead thoroughly.

Divide dough into 4 portions. Mix a few of the poppy seeds, if desired, into each portion.

Divide each portion into 3 smaller ones. Shape into rolls and place on a baking tray, lightly greased with margarine, to rise to double its volume.

Beat the egg with 1½ tbsp of water to make an egg wash. When rolls have risen by two-thirds, brush evenly with egg wash. Sprinkle with poppy seeds.

When rolls have risen fully, bake in an oven preheated to 220ºC for 10-12 minutes.

Transfer to a wire rack to cool. Brush the bread rolls lightly with oil.

Variations: Other flavourings and toppings that can be used are saffron, very finely chopped onion, rolled oats, caraway seeds, sesame seeds, herbs, very finely chopped walnuts or raisins, lemon zest, very finely chopped sun-dried tomatoes.

ର Crusty Bread Loaf

INGREDIENTS

25 g butter
10 g sugar
1 egg
225 g refined flour / maida
10 g yeast
100 ml water
20 ml milk
10 g salt
20 g margarine for greasing
20 ml milk for brushing
4 tsp oil for brushing

METHOD

Make a bread dough as given for dinner rolls alongside, using all the ingredients, except margarine, and milk and oil for brushing.

Knead to make a smooth dough, then leave to rise under a damp cloth for 10-15 minutes, till double in volume.

Knead again and shape into a 14" sausage.

Place the dough on a baking tray, greased with margarine. Keep it covered under a damp cloth for 10-15 minutes, till double in volume.

Brush dough with milk and score the top with a sharp knife. Sprinkle water on top.

Bake in an oven preheated to 225°C for about 30 minutes. Spray the oven with water after 5 minutes of baking.

Remove from the oven and brush the top with oil. Turn out on to a wire rack to cool.

Note: Depending on the gluten content, the strength of flour varies. So you may need a little more moisture to get the right consistency in the dough.

Variation: Crusty Bread Rolls: Divide the dough into 12 rolls after the first rising and follow the same procedure.

Hot Cross Buns

INGREDIENTS

30 g yeast
75 ml warm water
75 ml warm milk
50 g sugar
50 g butter
½ tsp vanilla essence
½ tsp salt
A pinch of freshly grated nutmeg
500 g flour
2 eggs, lightly beaten
50 g dried blackcurrants
50 g seedless raisins
1 tbsp margarine for greasing
1 egg yolk

Cross
50 g of flour

METHOD

In a large mixing bowl, dissolve the yeast in warm water and milk.

Add sugar, butter, vanilla, salt, nutmeg and half the flour. Whisk it to a smooth paste, gradually adding the eggs.

Stir in the dried fruit and remaining flour and knead to make a soft dough.

Dust a clean bowl with flour, place the dough in it and cover with a damp cloth.

Leave to rise till double in volume.

Turn the dough out on to a lightly floured surface and punch it down. Divide into 15 equal potions.

Shape into rolls and leave to rise on a baking tray, well greased with margarine. Cover and set aside till it rises to double its size.

Mix 50 g of flour for the cross with 2-3 tbsp of water to make a firm dough. Roll out and cut into strips.

Beat the egg yolk with 2 tbsp of water and brush the egg wash over the rolls. Gently press 2 strips of stiff dough on top of each roll in the form of a cross.

Bake the buns in an oven preheated to 220°C for 12-15 minutes.

Transfer to a wire rack to cool.

Note: Hot cross buns are traditionally served on Good Friday (the Friday before Easter) and during the Lenten season, but are good at any time.

ARROZ (RICE)

Cooking Rice

The cooking of rice is a delicate procedure and the foundation of several dishes. The variety of rice grain is also a matter of consideration. To match the right grain with the right cooking technique is often at times a matter of trial and error.

Hot Water Method

This process involves cooking long-grained rice, be it white or brown, in large quantities of water. The water is first brought to a boil, the salt added, and then the rice. It is left to simmer uncovered till the rice is tender. When done, the rice is strained, draining off excess starch. It is then returned to the pan and a few spoonfuls of butter are placed on the top.

Absorption Method

This method works best with basmati and short-grained rice. It involves cooking the rice in a measured quantity of water, which gets completely absorbed. The ideal measurement is 2½ parts water to 1 part rice.

Wash the rice and soak it in water for a while. Drain off and discard the water. Place fresh measured water, salt and rice in a pan and bring it to a boil. Lower the heat, cover the pan and cook for about 15 minutes, till the rice is tender. Turn off the heat and allow it to stand for a further 10 minutes. Using a fork, fluff up the rice grains.

Pilaf or Pulao

Pilaf or pulao and biryani are cooked using the absorption method. A pilaf constitutes a main dish with the addition of meat, poultry or vegetable. In this instance, the quantity of water is twice that of the rice. Rinse and wash the rice in cold water. Stand the rice in water for 1 hour before discarding the water. In a pan, sauté onions in oil sometimes along with other spices. Add the rice and sauté briefly, before adding hot boiling water or stock. When it reaches boiling point, cover and cook over low heat for 15 minutes.

ல Arroz com Coco

INGREDIENTS

2 cups rice
3 tbsp oil
1 onion, finely chopped
½ tsp black peppercorns
2-3 bay leaves / tej patta
5 green cardamoms
5 cloves
1" stick cinnamon
A pinch of saffron strands
½ tsp salt
900 ml chicken stock (p. 200)
100 ml thick coconut milk (p. 34)

METHOD

Wash the rice and soak in water for 1 hour.

In a pan, heat the oil and sauté the onion over moderate heat, till translucent.

Add the spices and sauté them for a few minutes.

Drain rice and add to the pan with the remaining ingredients.

Bring to a boil, lower heat and simmer till the rice is cooked.

᧰ Arroz de Mariscos

INGREDIENTS

2 cups rice
500 g mussels
500 g clams
4 medium tomatoes
100 ml olive oil
2 medium onions, finely chopped
4 garlic flakes, finely chopped
2 bay leaves / tej patta
1 tbsp tomato purée
1 tsp salt
1 tsp black pepper powder
A pinch of saffron strands
1 litre fish stock (p. 200)

Garnish
2 sprigs of fresh parsley, chopped

METHOD

Wash the rice and soak in water for 1 hour.

Scrub and wash mussels and clams well.

Plunge them separately into hot water for about 10 seconds.

Drain and discard any that have not opened.

Shell half the mussels and half the clams and discard the shells.

Blanch tomatoes, peel them and discard the seeds. Chop tomato flesh and set aside.

In a pan, heat the oil and sauté onions and garlic over moderate heat, till golden brown.

Add bay leaves and tomato purée and give it a stir. Stir in salt, pepper and saffron.

Drain the rice and add to the pan. Sauté briefly and pour in hot stock. Bring to a boil, lower heat and simmer till the rice is almost cooked.

Add clams, mussels and tomatoes. Stir them in gently.

Simmer for 10 minutes and serve garnished with parsley.

∾ Arroz de Galliano

INGREDIENTS

1¼ cups rice
1 kg chicken
1 tsp garlic paste
1 tsp ginger paste
100 ml olive oil
1 onion, finely chopped
4 garlic flakes, finely chopped
½" piece of ginger, finely chopped
4 medium tomatoes, chopped
3 green cardamoms
300 ml chicken stock (p. 200)
5-7 cloves
1" stick cinnamon
200 g mushrooms
250 g French beans
1 tsp salt
1 tsp freshly ground black pepper
3-4 sprigs of fresh parsley,
chopped

METHOD

Wash the rice and soak in water for 1 hour.

Clean and joint the chicken, wash and pat dry.

Combine garlic and ginger pastes in a bowl and
rub into chicken.

In a pan, heat the oil and sauté the chicken over
moderate heat, till brown.

Remove chicken from pan and keep aside in a
casserole dish.

Add onion and chopped garlic and ginger to
pan and sauté over moderate heat, till pale gold.

Drain rice, add to pan and sauté till evenly
browned.

Stir in the remaining ingredients.

Bring to a boil and spoon contents of pan over
the chicken in the casserole.

Cover the dish with foil.

Cook in an oven preheated to 175ºC for 1 hour.

ᘐ Arroz de Camarao

INGREDIENTS

2 cups rice
1 kg prawns
3 tbsp oil
1 medium onion, finely chopped
1" stick cinnamon
5 cloves
5 green cardamoms
½ tsp black peppercorns
2-3 bay leaves / tej patta
900 ml chicken stock (p. 200)
A pinch of saffron strands
½ tsp salt

Garnish
4 tbsp fresh coriander leaves,
chopped

METHOD

Wash the rice and soak in water for 1 hour.

Shell and de-vein the prawns. Wash well and set aside to drain.

In a pan, heat the oil and sauté the onion over moderate heat, till translucent.

Add the whole spices and bay leaves and sauté them for a few minutes.

Drain the rice and add to pan with stock, saffron and salt.

Bring to a boil, lower heat and simmer, till rice is three-quarters cooked.

Gently stir in prawns and simmer till rice and prawns are cooked.

Garnish with coriander leaves.

‍‍‍ Arroz Refogade

INGREDIENTS

1 cup rice
250 g mutton on the bone
2 tbsp olive oil
150 g bacon, diced
1 medium onion, finely sliced
1" stick cinnamon
150 g ham, diced
3 medium tomatoes, diced
500 ml mutton stock (p. 199)
30 g butter

Garnish
59 g seedless raisins

METHOD

Wash the rice and soak in water for 1 hour.

Wash mutton, cut it into cubes and boil it separately, till tender. Drain and set aside.

In a pan, heat the oil and fry bacon over moderate heat, till cooked. Drain and remove bacon from pan. Set aside.

Add onion to pan and sauté over moderate heat, till golden brown. Remove half the onion and set aside.

Add cinnamon and sauté briefly.

Drain rice and add to pan. Toss gently. Stir in the meat, bacon, ham and tomatoes and mix well.

Add hot stock, bring to a boil, lower heat and simmer till rice is tender.

Top pulao with butter and serve garnished with raisins and reserved fried onions.

๑ Arroz Pulao

INGREDIENTS

500 g basmati rice
100 ml ghee / oil
100 g seedless raisins
100 g cashew nuts
2 large onions, finely sliced
7 cloves
2 x 1" sticks cinnamon
5 green cardamoms
1 litre chicken stock (p. 200)
1 tsp salt
1 tsp black pepper powder

Garnish
2 hard-boiled eggs, sliced
50 gms seedless raisins
50 gms any nuts

METHOD

Wash the rice and soak in water for 1 hour.

In a pan, heat 1-2 tbsp ghee / oil and toss raisins and nuts over moderate heat for 1 minute. Drain and remove from pan. Set aside.

Add remaining ghee / oil to pan and heat through. Sauté onions over moderate heat, till golden brown. Remove half the onions and set aside.

Add whole spices to pan and toss for a moment.

Drain rice and add to pan. Stir briefly and pour in hot stock. Add salt and pepper and bring to a boil. Lower heat and simmer till rice is tender.

Garnish with hard-boiled eggs, raisins, nuts and reserved fried onions.

PICKLES AND CHUTNEYS

✍ Kasundi

INGREDIENTS

500 g cauliflower
225 g carrots
12 green chillies
500 ml groundnut oil
300 ml brown palm vinegar
1 tsp salt
1 tsp black pepper powder
Sugar to taste

Masala

3 tbsp cumin seeds
1 tsp mustard seeds
1 tsp fenugreek / methi seeds
½ tsp turmeric powder
A pinch of saffron strands
20 dried red Kashmiri chillies
75 ml brown palm vinegar

METHOD

Wash vegetables. Cut cauliflower in florets and dice the carrots and green chillies. Soak the vegetables in water.

Grind masala ingredients to a fine consistency with 75 ml of vinegar.

In a pan, using half the oil, fry the ground masala till the oil separates.

Pour remaining oil into pan and heat through. Add vegetables and sauté briefly.

Pour in 300 ml of vinegar and cook till it dries out.

Add salt and pepper, taste and add a little sugar to balance the flavours.

Cool and store in clean, sterilised glass jars for up to 6 months.

⚭ Wedding Pickle

INGREDIENTS

250 g carrots
1 raw papaya
2" piece of ginger
100 g sea salt
2 whole garlic heads
100 g green chillies
500 ml brown palm vinegar
25 g turmeric powder
100 g split mustard dal

METHOD

Cut carrots, papaya and ginger into fine juliennes.

Sprinkle with sea salt and dry out in the sun for 2 hours.

Clean garlic and remove the stalks from the chillies.

In a pan, pour in the vinegar. Add garlic and chillies and cook over moderate heat, till it comes to a boil. Remove from heat and cool.

Add turmeric powder, split mustard dal and prepared vegetables.

Store in a clean, sterilised glass jar for up to 6 months.

‫ Prawn Balchow

INGREDIENTS

500 g prawns (kardhi)
500 ml brown palm vinegar
4 tbsp oil
4-5 curry leaves
12 garlic flakes, finely chopped
2" piece of ginger, finely chopped
4-5 green chillies, finely chopped
1 tsp salt

Balchow Masala
11 dried red Kashmiri chillies
4 tbsp cumin seeds
2 tbsp mustard seeds
10 garlic flakes, roughly chopped
1" piece of ginger, roughly
chopped
1" piece turmeric or 1 tsp powder
A pinch of saffron strands
1 tbsp sugar

METHOD

Shell and de-vein the prawns. Wash well and drain thoroughly

Soak the prawns in vinegar for a few hours.

Grind masala ingredients to a fine consistency without water.

In a pan, heat the oil and sauté the curry leaves briefly over low heat.

Add garlic, ginger and green chillies and fry over low to moderate heat, till fragrant.

Mix in the ground masala and fry till the oil separates, and is a rich red-brown.

Add prawns, vinegar and salt and cook to a thick consistency.

Cool and store in clean, sterilised glass jars for up to 3-6 months.

๛ Shrimp Pickle

INGREDIENTS

750 g shrimp
2 sour limes
500 ml cider vinegar
4 bay leaves / tej patta
¼ tsp yellow mustard powder
¼ tsp powdered mace / javitri
1 tsp salt
1" piece of ginger, sliced in fine julienne
100 ml olive oil
1 medium onion, finely diced

Pickling spices
¼ tsp cinnamon sticks
¼ tsp green cardamoms
¼ tsp cloves

METHOD

Clean shrimp, wash and set aside to drain.

Poach the shrimp in lime juice for 10 minutes and set aside. Alternatively, cook them with the lime juice over low heat for 2-3 minutes.

Mix vinegar, bay leaves, mustard, mace and salt in a pan and bring to a boil.

Remove from heat and mix in ginger and pickling spices. Set aside till cool.

In another pan, heat the oil and sauté onion lightly. Pour contents of pan into the cooled vinegar-spice mix.

Add shrimp and refrigerate for 24 hours.

Store in clean, sterilised glass jars for up to 6 months.

❧ Aubergine Pickle

INGREDIENTS

2½ kg aubergine / baingan
1 litre brown palm vinegar
2 tbsp oil
50 g sesame seeds / til
50 g poppy seeds / khus-khus
150 g garlic paste
150 g ginger paste
1 tsp salt
100 g sugar

Masala

150 g green chillies, roughly
chopped
80 g dried red Kashmiri chillies
50 g cumin seeds
50 g mustard seeds
2 tsp fenugreek / methi seeds
1 tsp black pepper powder

METHOD

Wash and cube the aubergines.

Grind masala ingredients to a fine consistency, gradually adding a little of the measured vinegar, as required.

In a large pan, heat the oil and fry sesame and poppy seeds over low to moderate heat, till they splutter.

Add garlic and ginger pastes, stir briefly and mix in the ground masala.

Sprinkle in a little water if required, to prevent burning.

Stir in the aubergines and salt. Add sugar and vinegar and simmer till the oil floats to the surface.

Cool and store in clean, sterilised glass jars for up to 6 months.

ன Lime Pickle

INGREDIENTS

36 sour limes
250 g salt
750 ml white vinegar
250 g + 750 g sugar

METHOD

Wash limes and cut into halves. Remove seeds.

In a pan, place limes with 500 ml cold water and 2 tbsp of salt. Place pan on high heat and bring to a boil. Lower heat and simmer till the limes float to the top. Drain and set aside.

Dissolve remaining salt in vinegar.

In a heavy-bottomed pan, caramelise 250 gm of sugar, separately.

Remove pan from heat and let the bubbles subside. Add the vinegar mixture and remaining sugar to the caramel. Return pan to heat and boil it to a thick consistency, stirring frequently.

Add limes and bring to a boil. Cool and let it rest for 10 days before storing in clean, sterilised glass jars for up to 6 months.

๑ Green Chilli Pickle

INGREDIENTS

450 g green chillies
6 garlic flakes
1" piece of ginger
110 g tamarind
500 ml brown palm vinegar
1 cup sea salt
450 ml sesame seed oil
1 tsp mustard seeds
12 dried red Kashmiri chillies, kept whole
1 tsp turmeric powder
225 g sugar

METHOD

Wash the green chillies, dry them, and chop fine, along with the garlic and ginger.

Soak tamarind in 50-100 ml of the measured vinegar and extract the purée.

In a pan, put the tamarind purée, salt and 500 ml of water. Bring to a boil over high heat and remove from heat.

In another large pan, heat the oil and gently fry mustard seeds over low to moderate heat, till they splutter.

Add red chillies, ginger, garlic and turmeric. Stir for a few minutes and add sugar and tamarind juice.

Stir till thick and add the green chillies. Simmer for about 10 minutes.

Cool and store in clean, sterilised glass jars for up to 6 months.

∿ Salt Fish Chutney

Makes: 1½ kg

INGREDIENTS

100 g tamarind
30-60 ml + 30 ml brown palm
vinegar
900 g tomatoes
200 ml groundnut oil
2 tbsp poppy seeds / khus-khus
4-6 curry leaves
500 g dry salt fish

Masala
100 g garlic, roughly chopped
60 g ginger, roughly chopped
1 tsp red chilli powder
1 tsp turmeric powder
4-5 curry leaves

METHOD

Soak tamarind in 30-60 ml of vinegar for 1 hour. Extract the purée.

Blanch tomatoes in hot water. Remove and discard seeds and skin. Dice tomato flesh fine and set aside.

Grind masala ingredients to a fine consistency, gradually add 30 ml of vinegar.

In a pan, heat the oil and fry the poppy seeds over low to moderate heat, till they splutter.

Toss in curry leaves. Add the ground masala and fry well, till the oil separates.

Add tomatoes and fry for a while, till well blended.

Stir in the fish and tamarind purée and cook for about 10 minutes.

Cool and store in clean, sterilised glass jars for up to 6 months.

೫ Mango Chutney

INGREDIENTS

2½ kg raw, green mangoes
2 kg sugar
50 g garlic, crushed
50 g ginger, crushed
30 g red chilli powder
30 g salt
100 g seedless raisins
750 ml brown palm vinegar

METHOD

Peel the mangoes and remove and discard seeds. Slice mango flesh into fine julienne.

Dry them in the sun for 3 hours.

In a deep pan, add some water and mangoes and cook them with the sugar to a jam-like consistency over moderate to high heat.

Add garlic, ginger and chilli powder. Give it a stir.

Mix in salt, raisins and vinegar and cook for abour 1 hour over low to moderate heat, stirring continuously.

Cool and store in clean, sterilised glass jars for up to 1 month.

DESSERTS

๑ Semolina Sweet

INGREDIENTS

500 g semolina / rava / sooji
250 ml ghee
250 g sugar
100 g coconut, finely ground
150 ml rose water

Decoration
100 g almonds, blanched, peeled
and flaked

METHOD

In a pan, melt the ghee and roast the semolina lightly. Remove from heat and set aside.

In another pan, cook the sugar with 50 ml of water over very low heat, to a soft-ball, 115°C on the thermometer. (Alternatively, dip a teaspoon in the syrup and dip it in ice-cold water; you should be able to form the syrup into a soft ball.)

Add the coconut and semolina and stir in the rose water. Cook over low heat, stirring all the while, till the mix is almost dry.

Turn it out on to a lightly greased tray. Level the top and decorate with almonds.

Cut into diamond shapes when cool.

- -

๑ Alva de Grao

Makes: 24 pieces

INGREDIENTS

450 g whole Bengal gram / kala chana
225 g chopped almonds
75 ml rose water
100 g caster sugar
50 g ghee

METHOD

Boil the gram till soft. Drain and grind it fine to make a smooth paste. Place all the ingredients in a heavy-bottomed pan with 1 litre of water.

Cook the mix over low heat, stirring continuously till it leaves the sides of the pan.

Remove the mix and spread it on a greased tray. Level the surface and cut it into diamonds or squares, while it is still warm.

Guava Cheese

Bolachas

Steamed Dumplings

Jackfruit Ice Cream

Custard Apple Ice Cream

Cordial

Marble Cake

Coconut Ice Cream

Chocolate Fudge

Vanilla Cream

Lemon Curd

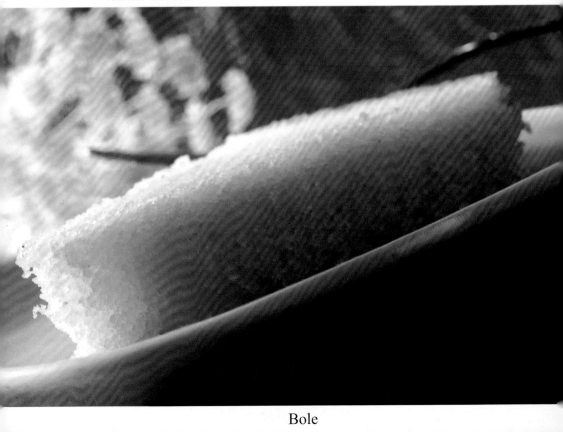

Bole

Fruit Salad

Melon and Ginger Sorbet

Kul-Kul

Macapao

Short Crust Pastry

Nankhaties

Khimad

Khimad Martini

Bombay Sunrise

Cherry Brandy

Peach Brandy

Khimad Mojito

Plum Brandy

Raisin Wine

೭ Macapao

INGREDIENTS

500 g almonds, blanched and peeled
1 kg sugar
150 ml rose water
1 egg white, stiffly beaten
1-2 tbsp ghee

METHOD

Powder the almonds and the sugar separately. (Another option is to grind the almonds with rose water to a smooth paste before adding it to the sugar.)

In a pan, dissolve the sugar in 50 ml of water over low heat.

Add the almond powder, rose water and stiffly beaten egg white.

Stir over gentle heat till the mixture starts to leave the sides of the pan.

Turn it out on to a lightly greased marble surface.

When cool enough to manage, knead the mix with the ghee.

When it is quite pliable, pull off small pieces of marzipan and form into shapes.(You can also use rubber moulds.)

Notes: Usually marzipan is shaped in fruit forms at Christmas and is made into Easter eggs, using a variety of food colours.

In India cashew nuts are used instead of almonds. When using whole almonds / cashew nuts blanch them and remove the skin.

ᕙ Bole de Grao

INGREDIENTS

400 g husked, split Bengal gram
/ chana dal
250 g butter
500 g sugar
7 eggs, separated
60 ml rose water
350 g semolina / rava / sooji
250 g fresh coconut, finely grated
1 tbsp butter for greasing

METHOD

Wash gram and soak in water for 1 hour. Drain.

Boil it in water till soft. Drain thoroughly and mash the gram.

In a round-bottomed bowl, cream butter and sugar, till light and fluffy.

Add egg yolks to creamed mix, a little at a time, whisking well after each addition, till incorporated. Whisk for a few minutes longer, till smooth.

Blend in rose water.

In a clean dry bowl, whisk egg whites to a stiff meringue (stiff peaks form when the whisk is raised).

Fold egg whites, gram and semolina alternately, a spoonful at a time into the creamed mixture. Set aside overnight.

Fold in coconut before baking.

Spoon batter into a cake tin lightly greased with butter. Bake in an oven preheated to 180°C for 5 minutes. Reduce the temperature to 150°C and bake for 50 minutes.

Test if done: a skewer inserted in the centre of the cake should come out clean. Bake for a few minutes longer, if required.

Remove from oven and turn out to cool on a wire rack before serving.

๑ Bole

Makes: 6" cake

INGREDIENTS

200 g butter
300 g sugar
5 eggs, separated
1 egg yolk
60 ml rose water
175 g semolina / rava / sooji
100 g fresh coconut, finely grated
1 tbsp butter for greasing

METHOD

Prepare the batter and bake the cake as given for Bole de Grao alongside.

- -

๑ Lemon Curd

Makes: 300 g

INGREDIENTS

50 g butter
80 g caster sugar
3 egg yolk
2 tbsp lemon / lime juice
½ tsp grated lemon / lime rind
6 baked tart shells

METHOD

Whisk butter and sugar over a double boiler, till tripled in volume. The mix should leave a trail when the whisk is raised.

In another pan, whisk egg yolks and lemon / lime juice and rind till it is pale in colour.

Add butter mix to the egg mix and return to the double boiler. Stir till the mixture coats the back of the spoon.

Cool and store in a refrigerator in a sterilised jar.

Use as a filling for tarts, cakes and pies, as and when required.

∽ Marble Cake

INGREDIENTS

250 g flour
1 tsp baking powder
240 g butter
1 tsp vanilla essence
240 g sugar
5 eggs, separated
30 g cocoa
20 g margarine for greasing

METHOD

Sift flour and baking powder together into a bowl.

In another bowl, cream butter, vanilla essence and sugar till light and fluffy.

Add egg yolks to creamed mix, a little at a time, whisking well after each addition, till incorporated. Whisk for a few minutes longer, till smooth.

In a clean dry bowl, whisk egg whites to a stiff meringue (stiff peaks form when the whisk is raised).

Fold egg whites into creamed mix, alternately with flour, a spoonful at a time.

Divide the batter into 2 portions. Add cocoa powder to one portion and mix well.

Spoon batters alternately into a lined and lightly greased 8" cake tin. Bake in an oven preheated to 150°C for 1 hour.

Test if done: a skewer inserted in the centre of the cake should come out clean. Bake for a few minutes longer, if required.

Remove cake from oven and allow to cool in the tin for 5 minutes before turning out on to a wire rack to finish cooling.

❧ Guava Cheese

INGREDIENTS

1 kg sugar
1 kg guava purée, strained
2 tbsp lime juice
½ tsp vanilla essence

METHOD

In a heavy-bottomed pan, cook the sugar with 50 ml of water over very low heat, to a soft-ball stage, 115°C on the thermometer. (Alternatively, dip a teaspoon in the syrup and dip it in ice-cold water; you should be able to form the syrup into a soft ball.)

In another pan, heat the guava purée.

Add purée to the sugar syrup with lime juice and vanilla essence.

Stir the mixture over low heat, till it is thick and begins to leave the sides of the pan.

Remove and pour on to a lightly greased tray. Level the surface.

Cut into squares when cool.

⌘ Gelea de Peras

INGREDIENTS

1 kg sugar
2 kg guava purée, strained
2 tbsp lime juice
½ tsp vanilla essence

METHOD

In a heavy-bottomed pan, boil the sugar with 50 ml of water to a softball stage, 115°C on the thermometer. (Alternatively, dip a teaspoon in the syrup and dip it in ice-cold water; you should be able to form the syrup into a soft ball.)

In another pan, heat the guava purée.

Add purée to the sugar syrup along with lime juice and vanilla essence.

Stir the mixture over low heat, till it has the consistency of jam.

Remove and pour it into a glass jar that can be sealed. Use within 3 months.

Variation: Gelea de Mangas (Mango Jelly) can be made in the same way with 2 kg of strained mango purée.

ꙮ Fou de Mel

INGREDIENTS

20 g yeast
20 ml milk
50 g + 500 g sugar
500 ml yoghurt, whisked smooth
500 g semolina / rava / sooji
4 eggs, lightly whisked
½ tsp vanilla essence

METHOD

In a large bowl, dissolve yeast with 50 g of sugar in the milk.

Add yoghurt and semolina to the yeast and stir in eggs and vanilla essence.

Set aside to prove for 3 hours, till the mix has a dropping consistency.

Grease a baking tray, which has individual shallow depressions, and heat it over a gas flame. Spoon batter into each depression. Turn the fou de mel when the base turns brown.

In a pan, put 500 g sugar and 500 ml water. Dissolve the sugar and boil to make a thick syrup.

Drop the cooked fou de mel into the syrup for a few minutes.

Remove and serve hot.

ᘒ Pancakes-1

INGREDIENTS

3 eggs, lightly beaten
A pinch of salt
100 g refined flour / maida
250 ml milk
15 g sugar
200 ml club soda
50 g clarified butter
Cornflour or icing sugar for
dusting

METHOD

Combine all the ingredients except the soda, clarified butter and dusting ingredient in a bowl. Mix to make a smooth batter.

(A bit of cornflour can be added to make it smoother.)

Rest the batter for 2 hours.

Add club soda, just before making the pancakes. Mix and add more water if required, to make a batter of pouring consistency.

Place a non-stick pan over moderate heat. When hot, brush the pan with clarified butter.

Prepare pancakes by pouring a spoonful of batter on to the heated pan.

Swirl batter towards the edges to get a lacy effect.

When the edges curl up, remove and place the pancake on a tray lightly dusted with cornflour or icing sugar.

Fill the pancake as required.

Notes: For savoury pancakes omit the sugar.
Fillings for pancakes are provided on p, 171.

ᕬ Pancakes-2

INGREDIENTS

15 g sugar
150 g flour
2 eggs, lightly beaten
300 ml milk
60 g butter (slightly browned)
1 tsp lime or orange zest
50 g clarified butter

METHOD

Prepare the batter and make the pancakes as given for pancakes-1. In this case there is no club ' soda that needs to be added before cooking them. Add more milk if required, to get a batter of pouring consistency.

೧ Fried Dumplings

INGREDIENTS

500 g whole wheat flour / atta
3-4 tbsp ghee
A pinch of a salt
Filling of choice (p. 171)
Oil for deep-frying

METHOD

On a large platter, mix all the ingredients, except the filling and oil.

Gradually add up to 200 ml of water and knead to make stiff but pliable dough. Add more water, if required. (If the dough is too soft, it will break while frying.)

Divide the dough into 24 portions.

Lightly grease your palm and flatten 1 portion into a disc. Place 1 tsp of filling in the centre.

Smear a little water along the edge of the disc to help seal it.

Then using your thumb, and index and middle fingers, pull up the sides to cover the filling. Let it taper to the top.

Seal well.

Make all dumplings in the same way.

Deep-fry the dumplings in batches, in hot oil, till golden brown.

Remove and place dumplings on a paper-lined colander to let excess oil drain off.

ൠ Steamed Dumplings

INGREDIENTS

400 ml water
2-3 tbsp oil
500 g rice flour
Filling of choice (p. 171)

METHOD

In a pan, bring the water to a boil then add the oil. Whisk in the rice flour.

Place the pan on a tava over very low heat.

Cover the pan and cook over very low heat, till you see steam coming out of the pan, about 10 minutes.

Turn the mixture on to a plate and while still hot, knead the mixture. Divide dough into 24 portions and fill and shape the dumplings as given alongside for fried dumplings.

Steam the dumplings for 10 minutes in a lightly greased steamer.

⟡ Kul-Kul

INGREDIENTS

1 kg semolina / rava / sooji
1 kg whole wheat flour / atta
250 ml milk
6 eggs, lightly beaten
500 ml ghee for deep frying
1 kg sugar

METHOD

Mix semolina and flour in a bowl. Add milk and eggs and mix well.

Gradually add up to 200 ml of water and knead to make a pliable dough. Add more water, if required. Set aside to rest overnight.

Take a small piece of dough, shape into an oval and pressing it against the teeth of an oiled comb, roll into a cylinder.

Deep-fry kul-kul in hot oil for a few minutes and remove while still white.

Cook the sugar for frosting with 30 ml of water over very low heat, to a soft-ball stage, 115°C on the thermometer. (Alternatively, dip a teaspoon in the syrup and dip it in ice-cold water; you should be able to form the syrup into a soft ball.)

Toss the cooked kul-kuls into the boiling sugar syrup and remove.

Turn out on to a stainless steel tray and allow the frosting to set.

Note: Tiny pieces of dough that are shaped and fried, then dipped in salt or sugar. Kul-kul are made especially at Christmas

᧡ Sweet Fillings for Pancakes, Nevris and Dumplings

For: 12 pancakes, nevris or dumplings

INGREDIENTS

Honey Raisin Filling
50 g seedless raisins
1 tbsp rum
50 ml honey
200 g fresh coconut, finely grated
¼ tsp green cardamom powder

Sweet Coconut Filling
150 g jaggery, grated and softened
50 g seedless raisins
1 large fresh coconut, finely grated
¼ tsp green cardamom powder

Raisin and Poppy Seed Filling
250 g desiccated coconut / kopra, grated
2 tsp poppy seeds / khus-khus
25 g seedless raisins
50 g powdered sugar

Mava Filling
250 g mava / unsweetened milk solids
250 g powdered sugar

METHOD

Soak the raisins in rum.

Put a heavy-bottomed pan over gentle heat.

Add the honey. When warm, add raisins, coconut and cardamom powder. Cook till the mixture is semi-dry.

Put a heavy-bottomed pan over gentle heat. Add the jaggery. When it melts, add raisins, coconut and cardamom powder. Cook till the mixture is semi-dry.

Roast the coconut and the poppy seeds separately on a hot tava.

Transfer to a pan. Add raisins and sugar.

Cook till filling is golden brown, stirring continuously.

In a heavy-bottomed pan, mix the mava and sugar.

Cook the filling on low heat, till it is semi-dry.

Alternatively, cook the mava till it turns a light pink. Remove from heat and add the sugar.

᳅ Short Crust Pastry (Sweet)

Makes: a 6" tart tray or 6 pastry cup shells

INGREDIENTS

115 g refined flour / maida
60 g softened butter
60 g caster sugar
½ tsp vanilla essence
2 egg yolks, lightly beaten

METHOD

Work in a cool area.

Sift flour into a bowl to aerate it.

Cream butter with sugar, till light and fluffy.

Mix in vanilla essence and egg yolks.

Lightly fold in the flour.

Using fingertips helps keep the fat from the warmth of the hands. The texture of the mix should be sandy, more like breadcrumbs. Gently make into a ball and cover it with cling film to prevent it from drying out.

Remove from the refrigerator a few minutes before rolling it, to soften slightly.

Roll out as needed for pie bases, tart shells and barquettes (boat-shaped tarts).

If baking blind, line the pastry with foil and fill with beans before baking to prevent the pastry from rising up.

ᔈ Short Crust Pastry (Savoury)

Makes: a 6" tart tray or 8 pastry cup shells

INGREDIENTS

115 g refined flour / maida
60 g cold butter
1 egg yolk, lightly beaten

METHOD

Sift flour into a bowl to aerate it.

Crumble the fat into the flour using a dough cutter or a knife. The result should look like fine breadcrumbs.

Add egg yolk and gently make into a smooth ball.

Cover with cling film to prevent it from drying out. Rest the paste in the refrigerator before rolling and baking.

Remove from the refrigerator a few minutes before rolling it, to soften slightly.

Roll out as needed for pie bases, tart shells and barquettes (boat-shaped tarts).

Bake, as required.

- - - - - - - - - - - - - - - - -

ᔈ Cashew Nut Cream

Makes: 500 g

INGREDIENTS

225 g cashew nuts
50 ml rose water
300 ml milk
225 g sugar
60 g butter
¼ tsp vanilla essence

METHOD

Grind the nuts to a fine paste with rose water.

Place all the ingredients in a heavy-bottomed pan and stir continuously over low heat.

As the mixture starts to leave the sides of the pan, turn it out on to a lightly greased tray. Spread out and level the surface.

Score with a knife and cut while still warm.

175

❧ Chocolate Cream / Fudge

INGREDIENTS

1 litre milk
1 vanilla pod, split
450 g sugar
50 g cocoa
100 g butter
100 g walnuts, flaked

METHOD

In a heavy-bottomed pan, boil the milk with the vanilla pod, till reduced to half its original volume.

Stir continuously to avoid burning the milk at the bottom.

Remove vanilla pod and wash it for reuse.

Transfer the milk to a fresh heavy-bottomed pan.

Add the remaining ingredients. Stir over low heat.

As the mixture starts to leave the sides of the pan, turn it out on to a lightly greased tray. Spread out and level the surface.

Score with a knife and cut while still warm.

Note: If you can't get hold of a vanilla pod, add ½ tsp vanilla essence to the reduced milk with the remaining ingredients

∽ Empada de Coco e Semolina Makes: an 8" pie

INGREDIENTS

150 g sweet short crust pastry
(p. 172)
1½ cups semolina / rava / sooji
4 eggs, separated
1 cup sugar
1 large fresh coconut, grated
Grated rind and juice of 1 lime
¼ tsp cinnamon powder

METHOD

Line a 9" flan tin with short crust pastry.

Soak the semolina in 1½ cups of water for 30 minutes.

Cream egg yolks with sugar, till light and fluffy.

Fold in semolina, coconut and lime rind and juice.

Whisk egg whites till stiff peaks form when the whisk is raised.

Fold into the creamed mixture.

Spoon the mix into the prepared pastry flan.

Sprinkle with cinnamon powder.

Bake in an oven preheated to 175ºC-200ºC for 30 minutes.

෮ Orange & Honey Curd Tart

Makes: 2x6" tarts or 12x2" tarts

INGREDIENTS

225 g sweet short crust pastry
(p. 172)
250 g soft cottage cheese
50 g honey
2 tbsp orange flower water
300 ml orange juice
1 tsp cornflour
3 egg yolks, lightly beaten
150 ml cream, lightly whipped
1 egg white

Decoration

Icing sugar for dusting
A few mint leaves, kept whole
15 g candied orange zest

METHOD

Line tart moulds with short crust pastry.

In a bowl, crumble the cottage cheese and mix it with honey, orange flower water, orange juice, cornflour and egg yolks.

Fold in cream

In a clean dry bowl, whisk egg white to a stiff meringue (stiff peaks form when the whisk is raised) and fold it in.

Spoon into prepared tart moulds. Bake in an oven preheated to 200°C for 30 minutes.

Remove and cool.

Dust tarts with icing sugar, and decorate with mint leaves and orange zest.

⬿ Borose

INGREDIENTS

3 egg yolks, lightly beaten
400 g caster sugar
4 egg whites
300 g fresh coconut, finely
ground
400 g semolina / rava / sooji
30 g butter for greasing

METHOD

Beat egg yolks with sugar, till the sugar is dissolved.

In a clean dry bowl, whisk egg whites to a stiff meringue (stiff peaks form when the whisk is raised).

Fold a spoonful at a time into the yolk mixture alternately with coconut and semolina.

Set aside to rest overnight.

Divide dough into 24 portions and flatten them into round biscuits.

Arrange on a lightly greased and floured baking tray. Bake in an oven preheated to 150° for 40-45 minutes.

Remove and transfer to a wire rack to cool.

൭ Nevries

INGREDIENTS

1 kg whole wheat flour / atta
250 ml milk
Filling of choice (p. 171)
300 g ghee for deep-frying

METHOD

In a bowl, mix flour, milk and 300 ml of water and knead thoroughly to make a pliable dough. Set aside to rest overnight.

Divide dough into 24 portions and roll each into 3" round discs.

Place a spoonful of filling in the centre along one half.

Apply a little moisture along the edges. Fold over the top half to form a semicircle and seal.

Deep-fry in hot oil for a few minutes. Remove while still white or a very pale brown.

Place on a paper-lined colander to let excess oil drain off.

๑ Cordial

INGREDIENTS

800 g caster sugar
500 g fresh coconut, finely grated
150 ml rose water
¼ tsp pink food colour (optional)
2 egg whites, lightly beaten

METHOD

Dissolve the sugar in 100 ml water.

Boil the sugar to a soft-ball stage, 115°C on the thermometer. (Alternatively, dip a teaspoon in the syrup and dip it in ice-cold water; you should be able to form the syrup into a soft ball.)

Add the coconut, rose water and a few drops of food colouring (if used — pink is popular).

When the mixture starts to leave the sides of the pan, turn off the heat and stir in lightly beaten egg whites.

Fill into pre-baked tart shell made of short crust pastry (p.172) to make coconut baskets.

Alternatively, pour on to a lightly greased tray and level the surface. Cut into diamond shapes before the mixture cools.

∽ Vanilla Cream

Makes: 500 g

INGREDIENTS

100 g cashew nuts
400 g sugar
1 litre milk
1 vanilla pod, split
1 tbsp butter / ghee

METHOD

Grind the cashew nuts very fine with a little of the measured sugar.

In a heavy-bottomed pan, boil the milk with the vanilla pod, till reduced to half its original volume.

Stir continuously to avoid burning the milk at the bottom.

Remove vanilla pod and wash it for reuse.

Transfer the milk to a fresh deep-bottomed pan.

Add the cashew nuts and sugar and stir over moderate heat, till the mixture starts to leave the sides of the pan.

Transfer to a lightly greased marble slab and knead it with a spoonful of butter / ghee.

Before it cools completely, form into shapes using a rubber mould.

Note: If you can't get hold of a vanilla pod, add ½ tsp vanilla essence to the reduced milk with the remaining ingredients

๑ Bolachas

INGREDIENTS

3 egg whites
½ tsp vanilla essence
200 g caster sugar
450 g fresh coconut, grated
20 g refined flour / maida

METHOD

In a clean and dry bowl, whisk the egg whites and vanilla essence to a stiff meringue (stiff peaks form when the whisk is raised).

Continue whisking and gradually add the caster sugar in three stages.

Fold in coconut and flour.

Fill into a piping bag and pipe whorls on to a lined and greased baking tray.

Bake in an oven preheated to 150°C for 1 hour.

Turn off the oven and leave the macaroons inside, with the door open.

Allow the macaroons to dry out and complete the cooking process.

Remove when the bottom sounds hollow if tapped.

Place on a wire rack to cool completely

๑ Chocolate Macaroons

Makes: 12 macaroons

INGREDIENTS

50 g cocoa powder
150 g almonds, blanched, peeled
and ground
40 g refined flour / maida
8 egg whites
¼ tsp vanilla essence
300 g caster sugar

METHOD

Sift cocoa, ground almonds and flour together
into a bowl.

In a clean and dry bowl, whisk the egg whites
and vanilla essence to a stiff meringue (stiff
peaks form when the whisk is raised).

Continue whisking and gradually add the caster
sugar in three stages.

Fold in sifted ingredients.

Proceed as given for coconut macaroons
(p. 181).

- -

๑ Saffron & Mace Ice Cream

Makes: 500 g

INGREDIENTS

10 saffron strands
700 ml milk
6 egg yolks
275 g caster sugar
A pinch of powdered mace / javitri

METHOD

In a pan, put the saffron and milk and bring to a
boil over high heat. Remove from heat, but keep
the milk hot.

In a non-reactive bowl, cream egg yolks and
sugar till light and fluffy.

Whisk in hot milk. Transfer to a fresh pan.

Cook the mix over a double boiler till it coats the
back of a wooden spoon.

Remove, stir in the mace and cool.

Churn it in an ice cream machine and freeze.

∾ Yogurt Ice Cream

Makes: 1½ kg

INGREDIENTS

400 ml honey
800 ml thick yogurt
60 ml lime juice
100 g sugar

METHOD

Mix honey with yogurt, then combine the remaining ingredients.

Churn in an ice-cream machine and freeze.

- - - - - - - - - - - - - - - - - -

∾ Lemon Ice Cream

Makes: 500 g

INGREDIENTS

250 ml milk
250 ml cream
125 g sugar
6 egg yolks
Grated rind of 1 lemon or lime
2 tbsp lemon or lime juice

METHOD

In a clean pan, boil the milk and cream together.

Cream sugar and egg yolks together, till light and fluffy.

Whisk in the hot milk. Transfer to a fresh pan.

Place pan over a double boiler or a tava over low heat. Stir over gentle heat till the custard coats the back of the spoon.

Remove from heat and set aside till cool.

In a small pan, bring the lemon or lime rind and juice to a boil. Remove from heat, cool and add to the cooled custard.

Churn in an ice cream machine and freeze.

↬ Custard Apple Ice Cream

Makes: 1 kg

INGREDIENTS

500 ml milk
500 ml cream
1 vanilla pod, split
8 egg yolks
125 g sugar
500 g custard apple pulp

METHOD

In a pan, boil the milk and cream with the vanilla pod.

Whisk egg yolks and sugar till light and fluffy.

Whisk in hot milk and cream. Transfer to a fresh pan.

Place pan over a double boiler or a tava over low heat. Stir over gentle heat, till the custard coats the back of the spoon.

Remove the vanilla pod and when semi-cool add the custard apple pulp.

Churn it in an ice cream machine and freeze.

- -

↬ Jackfruit Ice Cream

Makes: 1 kg

INGREDIENTS

500 ml milk
500 ml cream
1 vanilla pod
8 egg yolks
125 g sugar
250 g ripe jackfruit flesh, finely chopped

METHOD

Prepare the custard as given above for custard apple ice cream.

Add the chopped jackfruit when it is semi-cool.

Churn in an ice cream machine and freeze.

๑ Coconut Ice Cream

Makes: 500 g

INGREDIENTS

250 ml cream
500 ml thick coconut milk (p. 34)
6 egg yolks
150 g sugar
2 tbsp malibu / rum

METHOD

Prepare the custard as given for custard apple ice cream alongside.

In this case, just heat the cream till it is about to boil.

Cool the custard and add the coconut milk and Malibu / rum.

Churn in an ice cream machine and freeze.

- -

๑ Chickoo Ice Cream

Makes: 1 kg

INGREDIENTS

500 ml milk
500 ml cream
1 vanilla pod
8 egg yolks
125 g sugar
250 g chickoo purée

METHOD

Prepare the custard as given for custard apple ice cream alongside.

Cool the custard and add the chickoo purée.

Semi-set in a freezer.

Remove and churn in an ice cream machine. Freeze.

ബ Sorbet Syrup

INGREDIENTS

1½ kg sugar
1½ litres water
200 g liquid glucose

METHOD

In a large pan, heat all the ingredients together and bring it to a boil. Simmer for 2 minutes, till sugar has dissolved.

Use to make sorbets.

- -

ബ Melon and Ginger Sorbet

Makes: 500 g

INGREDIENTS

450 g cleaned musk melon flesh
1 tbsp lime juice
170 g brown sugar
280 ml cream
50 g crystallised ginger, finely chopped

METHOD

Purée the melon flesh and strain.

Add lime juice and sugar to the purée and leave the mixture for 2 hours.

Whip the cream and fold into the melon purée with crystallised ginger.

Churn in an ice cream machine and freeze.

ꙮ Lychee Sorbet

INGREDIENTS

100 g lychees, seeded and kept
whole
500 g lychee purée
400 ml sorbet syrup (p. 186)

METHOD

Peel and chop the whole lychees.

In a pan, cook the lychees and purée in sorbet syrup for 10 minutes. Cool and freeze. Remove and whisk to break any icicles.

Churn in an ice cream machine.

- -

ꙮ Green Mango Sorbet

INGREDIENTS

500 g raw green mango
250 ml sorbet syrup (p. 186)
250 g sugar
1 litre water
2 tbsp lime juice

Decoration
Zest of 1 lemon
1 tsp sugar
A few mint leaves, kept whole

METHOD

Peel green mangoes and slice. Place the mangoes in a large pan with the remaining ingredients, except the decoration.

Bring to a boil, lower heat and simmer for about 30 minutes.

Remove from heat and cool.

Mash and strain the pulp.

Churn in an ice cream machine and freeze.

Cook the lemon zest with sugar for a minute, over very low heat. Cool and cut into fine strips.

Serve the sorbet in tall glasses decorated with mint leaves and candied lemon.

ॐ Guava Sorbet

INGREDIENTS

100 g glucose
700 ml sorbet syrup (p. 186)
700 ml guava purée, strained
1 tbsp lime juice

METHOD

Boil glucose and sorbet syrup together and cool.

Stir in the guava purée and lime juice.

Churn in an ice cream machine and freeze.

ॐ Tamarind & Ginger Sorbet

INGREDIENTS

3" piece of ginger, grated
600 ml sorbet syrup (p. 186)
100 g tamarind purée (p. 34)
8 green cardamoms
175 ml cream
4 tbsp brandy

METHOD

In a pan, put the ginger, sorbet syrup, tamarind purée and cardamoms. Place over high heat and boil for 5 minutes.

Strain and semi-freeze.

Whisk cream and brandy and fold it into the semi-frozen syrup.

Churn in an ice cream machine and refreeze.

ALCOHOL

Wine and liquor have always played an important role in the diet of the people of north Konkan. Toddy, a mild sweet liquor obtained by tapping the (tadh) palm tree, *caryota urens* and arrack from *cocos nucifera* used to be drunk mid-morning to fortify the farm and plantation workers against fatigue. Now known as toddy, this liquor was once called Maria Branca. Neera is what it is called just before it has been allowed to ferment. Neera is sweet, and best consumed early in the day.

Liquor is distilled with skill and in different strengths, the more popular one being khimad, a spiced, sweetened liquor, with coconut liquor as its base. Khimad is made from the spirit which is the first distil and so is smoother than feni which is not as popular and is double distilled. The liquor is pure and unadulterated and great value is put to its medicinal properties.

The wealthy stored the prepared khimad in wooden casks. Liquor is heated in earthenware jars with narrow necks, served hot in small earthen cups known as cheuvnies. Socially, liquor plays an important role both on sad occasions and for joyous celebrations, and no function is considered complete without it being served.

Toddy, also suggestively called the 'poor man's beer', was drunk by the natives. Despite its alcoholic content, it is very nutritious and is consumed early in the morning before heading off to work in the fields.

⤶ Khimad

INGREDIENTS

750 ml neutral liquor / gin / vodka / tequila
4 tbsp sugar
6 green cardamoms
1" stick cinnamon
6 cloves
1 tea bag

METHOD

In a non-reactive pan, boil 250 ml of liquor with sugar and 200 ml of water.

Crush the spices coarsely and add to the pan with the tea bag. Set aside to steep for a while.

Add to the remaining alcohol.

Reheat before serving and serve warm.

Note: The neutral liquor used here is the local country-made liquor which is home-distilled. There is also a variety that is commercially available (extra neutral alchohol). Gin, vodka or tequila may be used, as it has no flavour.

⤶ Khimad Mojito

Serves: 1

INGREDIENTS

5-6 mint leaves
30 ml khimad (p. 191)
30 ml lime juice
30 ml club soda or lemonade

Garnish
1 mint leaf, kept whole

METHOD

Put mint leaves into a glass. Crush or muddle the leaves with a spoon or crusher.

Pour in the khimad. Add lime juice and club soda or lemonade.

Top with ice cubes and stir well

Garnish with a rinsed fresh mint leaf.

໑ Khimad Martini

INGREDIENTS

30 ml khimad (p. 191)
30ml Gordon's Dry Gin
50 g ice

METHOD

Put all ingredients into a cocktail shaker.

Stir well or give it a good shake.

Strain into a martini glass.

----

໑ Bombay Sunrise

Serves: 1

INGREDIENTS

30 ml khimad (p. 191)
30 ml white rum
180 ml orange juice
15 ml grenadine
10 ml sugar syrup
50 g ice

METHOD

Put all ingredients in a cocktail shaker.

Stir well or give it a good shake.

Pour into a tall (Tom Collins) glass.

ଚ Khimad Twist

INGREDIENTS

60 ml khimad (p. 191)
A twist of orange or lemon peel

METHOD

Pour khimad into a shot glass.

With a lighter, set one end of the peel on fire. This extracts flavourful oils.

Drop it into the drink. Be careful not to set the drink on fire!

Drink neat.

ଚ Vino de Gengibre

Makes: 1-2 litres

INGREDIENTS

250 g ginger, finely chopped
2 x 1" cinnamon sticks
10 cloves
5 dried red chillies, seeded
1 kg sugar
Juice of 6 limes
50 g yeast
200 ml rum

METHOD

In a pan, bring 4 litres of water to a boil. Add the ginger along with the spices and sugar. Lower heat and simmer for 1 hour.

Add the lime juice and leave to cool. Strain.

Dissolve the yeast in 50 ml of water and add to the cooled liquid in the pan.

Transfer contents of pan to a clay jar. Seal the jar with a muslin cloth and lid. Let it stand for a fortnight to allow the sediment to settle.

Strain carefully, without disturbing the sediment.

Stir in rum. Transfer to bottles and serve after a month.

∾ Raisin Wine

INGREDIENTS

1 kg black raisins
2 kg sugar
15 g yeast
200 g wheat grains, crushed

METHOD

Mince the raisins.

In a large bowl, dissolve the yeast in 50 ml of water and add raisins and sugar. Pour in 4 litres of water.

Add the crushed wheat. Store for 15 days stirring once a day.

Strain and store for a week, to allow the wine and sediment to settle.

Strain again and transfer to bottles.

Serve chilled.

- -

∾ Cherry Brandy

INGREDIENTS

1 kg fresh cherries
500 g sugar
1" stick cinnamon
A pinch of allspice / kabab chini
1 vanilla pod
1 litre brandy

METHOD

Wash the cherries and place them in a jar.

In a pan, dissolve sugar over low heat in 100 ml of water, along with the spices and vanilla pod.

Pour the sugar syrup and brandy over the cherries and leave for 25 days before use.

Use the cherries separately in desserts.

∾ Plum Brandy

Makes: 1½ litres

INGREDIENTS

1 kg plums
500 g sugar
4 cloves
1" stick cinnamon
¼ tsp allspice / kabab chini
1 vanilla pod
1 litre brandy

METHOD

Proceed as given for cherry brandy (p. 194).

Leave for 1 month before use.

Use the plums separately, topped with ice cream or whipped cream.

- -

∾ Peach Brandy

Makes: 1½ litres

INGREDIENTS

1 kg peaches
500 g sugar
1" stick cinnamon
1 vanilla pod
¼ tsp allspice / kabab chini
1 litre brandy

METHOD

Proceed as given for cherry brandy (p. 194).

Leave for 1 month before use.

Use the peaches separately topped with ice cream or whipped cream.

‿ Vinho de Seiva de Coqueiro

INGREDIENTS

250 g large black raisins
2 bottles sweet toddy
400 g sugar
Juice of 1 sour lime

METHOD

Wash the raisins well and dry them thoroughly. Chop fine and place them in a large jar.

Add the toddy and sugar along with lime juice.

Stir till the sugar dissolves.

Seal the jar with a thick cloth and removing it once a day, stir the mixture.

After 10 days, strain the mixture through a muslin cloth without disturbing the sediment at the bottom.

Allow it to stand for a week before straining the wine again and storing it in glass bottles.

Stopper the bottles and serve after a week.

STOCKS

As in several cuisines, the preparation of stocks takes absolute priority. To get the perfect stock, it is essential to purchase the right ingredients and not skimp on quality. They play an integral role in giving a dish its body and character. Good soups and sauces rely considerably on a good stock. The procedures in obtaining a good stock are simple, and with a watchful eye over it, produce wonders.

A style humbly borrowed for non-vegetarian stocks is the Asian way of first blanching bones then cracking them in order to get the most out of them by way of flavour and nutrients.

Careful washing of vegetables and their preparation is essential before use. Stocks should be skimmed occasionally to remove scum, froth and impurities. It is important to regulate heat, as boiling results in a cloudy stock. Time spent on preparation is also necessary to obtain a rich and full-bodied stock.

- -

ꙮ Vegetable Stock (Brown)

Makes: 1 litre

INGREDIENTS

2 medium onions
225 g tomatoes
2 carrots
225 g red pumpkin / kaddu
1" piece of ginger
1 sprig mint leaves
50 g masoor dal
2 tbsp ghee
1¼ litres water
4 black peppercorns
Salt to taste

METHOD

Slice onions and tomatoes. Wash and roughly chop the other vegetables. Wash masoor dal separately.

In a pan, heat the ghee and sauté onions and tomatoes over moderate heat, till lightly browned.

Add the remaining ingredients, except salt.

Simmer for an hour, stirring occasionally.

Mash vegetables to a pulp. Strain. Set aside the liquid stock.

Add one cup of water to the pulp, mash with a ladle and simmer again.

Strain into the previous stock.

Add salt sparingly.

∾ Vegetable Stock (White)

INGREDIENTS

225 g white pumpkin / doodhi
1 small cucumber
225 g cabbage
1 medium onion
1" piece of ginger
1 sprig of mint leaves
8 black peppercorns
6 cloves
1 litre water
Salt to taste

METHOD

Wash and cut the vegetables and ginger. Coarsely crush the peppercorns and cloves

In a large pan, add all the ingredients except salt. Simmer for 1 hour.

Strain the stock through a fine muslin or strainer.

Add salt sparingly.

- -

∾ Beef / Mutton Stock

Makes: 1 litre

INGREDIENTS

3 kg beef / veal / mutton bones
1 kg meat knuckle (for beef stock)
2 medium onions, roughly chopped
2 carrots, roughly chopped
2 leeks, roughly chopped
30 g tomato purée
8 peppercorns
3 litres water

METHOD

Wash the bones and put them in a roasting pan with the onions, carrots, leeks and tomato purée. Roast in an oven preheated to 225ºC for about 45 minutes to brown well.

Put all the ingredients into a pan. Gently simmer for 3-4 hours, skimming occasionally.

Strain and de-fat the stock using tissue or absorbent paper.

Variation: White Beef / Veal / Mutton Stock: Do not brown the bones and vegetables and omit the tomato purée.

ᕔ Fish Stock

INGREDIENTS

450 g bones of any white fish
45 g butter
3 medium onions, chopped
1 celery stalk, roughly chopped
1 bay leaf / tej patta
10 black peppercorns
1 bouquet garni (p. 203)
1 litre water

METHOD

Rinse and chop the bones.

In a pan, melt butter over gentle heat and sauté onions for 2 minutes.

Add the remaining ingredients.

Bring the soup to a boil, lower heat and simmer for 20 minutes.

Skim off any froth and scum.

Strain the stock through a fine muslin or strainer.

ᕔ Chicken Stock

Makes: 1½ litres

INGREDIENTS

2 kg chicken bones
3 medium onions
4 cloves
10 peppercorns
6 garlic flakes
4 sprigs of parsley
3 carrots, roughly chopped
3 stalks of celery, roughly chopped
1 bouquet garni (p. 203)
3 litres water

METHOD

Wash the bones and crack them lightly. Push the cloves into the onions.

Cut the onions in half.

Put all ingredients into a pan and bring to a boil.

Lower heat and simmer for 2 hours skimming the top occasionally.

Strain the stock through a fine muslin or strainer.

SPICES AND HERBS

Spices and herbs play a vital role in many cuisines around the world, more so in the cuisines of South East Asia and India. India has been both a producer and consumer of spices for thousands of years. The character and importance of spices are of absorbing interest. Sanskrit writings of about three thousand years ago emphasise their value as preservatives and as being rich in medicinal properties. Ayurveda, the ancient art of Hindu medicine, lists a whole range of herbs and spices in the cure of various ailments.

Spices through the centuries were used primarily to preserve, as seasoning and for medicinal value. Modern-day use concerns itself mainly with flavour and taste. Some traditions remain, however. Lentils and peas are cooked with a bit of ginger or asafoetida to counteract flatulence.

There are no hard and fast rules concerning the use of spices and an innate chef's sense suggests which spices lend themselves to different aspects of cooking. Spices which are too strong or flavoursome are avoided in sweets; turmeric is used in small quantities, and only in dishes that allow its flavour to mellow. Chillies play an important role in Latin American and Asian cuisines. They need to be handled with care as their oils irritate the eyes and skin. Oiled hands or gloves are advisable when working with chillies.

The combination of spices in a dish is important for flavour, texture and colour. The aroma of certain spices is tantalising; they take precedence over others, and give a dish a distinction of its own – for example, cinnamon when used in pulaos and pies.

Preserving & Storing Herbs & Spices

Spices and herbs are at their flavoursome best in the summer months. In India, late summer is the ideal time for drying and preserving them and extracting their essential oils. Some of the imported herbs like bay, basil and thyme dry well if hung in small bunches in a warm, airy place away from direct sunlight. Bunches of onions and garlic are dried in India in this manner. The dried leaves, stems or pods need to be stored in airtight containers in a cool and dry area. Herbs like basil, chive, dill, fennel and parsley lose much of their flavour when dried, but freeze well.

Flavourful herbs like basil, thyme, tarragon and rosemary can be infused in bottles of oil or vinegar for use in salad dressings and marinades when fresh herbs are not available. This creation of flavouring oils in India has been done only with chilli and pepper so far and mostly used in tempering.

Preserving Herbs in Vinegar

This is suitable for basil, chive, bay, garlic, sage, rosemary or thyme. Take a heaped teaspoon of fresh herb with a bruised clove of garlic and place in a jar that can be sealed. Heat two cups of vinegar to simmering point. Pour the hot vinegar into the jar. Seal tightly and keep for two weeks, shaking occasionally. Strain vinegar and transfer to a clean bottle. A fresh sprig of herb adds a nice touch before sealing the bottle.

Preserving Herbs in Oils

Place fresh herbs in a jar that can be sealed. Add good quality olive oil. Choose one or more of the following herbs: basil, chive, bay, garlic, sage, rosemary or thyme. Other options are red or green chillies, black peppercorns and strips of lemon, lime or orange peel. Herb-flavoured oils are great with pastas and grilled foods, as well as for salad dressings.

Preserving herbs in oil or vinegar make a great gift for a friend. These jars or bottles lend colour to one's kitchen shelf or table.

Classic Herb Combinations

The most famous combination is a *bouquet garni*, which comprises a bunch of parsley, a thyme sprig, and a bay leaf or two that are tied together. It is used to flavour dishes which require a long process of cooking. The herbs are tied into the hollow of a celery stalk.

Spice Care

Spices are bought whole as berries, buds, bark, etc. This allows for the retention of flavour and pungency far longer than powdered spices. Methods of preparation of spices vary, and are all aimed at bringing out the maximum flavour.

Dry-roasting is a process of heating a heavy-bottomed pan, then adding the spices and cooking them for 2-3 minutes, while shaking the pan continuously to prevent burning. The spices are then ground fine, usually with a mortar and pestle.

Another method of processing spices is by frying them in oil. The pan is first heated, and the oil poured in. When the oil is quite hot, the spices are added. At times, this method is used to infuse and flavour oils, by removing the spices after cooking.

Spices are best ground just before use or a day or two prior. Grinding releases oils, flavours and aromas. A few spices like mace, ginger, cinnamon and turmeric are bought in the ground form as they are hard to grind at home. Fresh spices like ginger, garlic and chillies are best ground using mortar and pestle.

The most familiar method is that of shredding and chopping the spices fine. This process is usually carried out for fresh spices like garlic and ginger and herbs. Some spices, namely ginger, horseradish and nutmeg are also grated before use. Nutmeg needs to be grated on the smallest part of the grater. Another method of releasing the flavours of spices like lemon grass, ginger, cardamom and garlic is by crushing or bruising. Cardamom is crushed using mortar and pestle. Infusions are carried out by placing spices into warm liquids before being used; saffron and tamarind are two commonly used spices for which this method is used.

Allspice (*Pimenta dioica*) Kabab Chini

This pea-sized fruit, a native of the West Indies, has a flavour and aroma which is a blend of cinnamon, nutmeg, peppercorns and cloves. Its volatile oil is known as Eugenol. Exports are mainly from Jamaica, where the plant grows in a semi-wild state. The preservative properties of allspice were valued by the seventeenth century seafarers, and are still widely used by the fishing industry in Scandinavia. It is used whole in pickles, gravies and meat preparation. Ground, it is added to baked products, namely biscuits and Christmas puddings, and relishes and pickles. It is a primary ingredient in a West Indian liqueur called pimento dram or Jamaica dram. The whole berries are an ingredient in mulled wine and in the liqueurs, Benedictine and Chartreuse. The whole or ground spice is used to flavour pickles and chutneys. Ideally, buy the whole spice and grind it as and when required, as it loses its strength soon.

Anise (*Pimpinella anisum*) Badishep / Saunf

The fruit of a small plant found in southern Europe, Tunisia, India and Chile, anise is a member of the parsley family. It is often used to flavour liquorice. Lacy and limber in texture, the leaves are seldom used. Common in seed form, it is one of the many non-descriptive herbs. Ground, it is used in fish soups, sauces, rye bread, coffee, cakes, cookies and candies, and is the main ingredient in the manufacture of the liqueur, Anisette. It is also an ingredient in other flavoured drinks such as the Spanish ojen, Turkish raki, Greek ouzo and Arab arrak. Its ability to counteract indigestion was realised by the Romans, who served a spice cake containing anise after their gastronomic parties. In India, anise is eaten as a mouth freshener and is a handy cure for hiccups.

Asafoetida (*Ferula asofoetida*) Hing

Resembling wild cow parsley, this spice is native to Afghanistan, but has adapted itself to Indian soil. Afghans cook it whole as a vegetable but the main ingredient is the sap, which is dried and ground to a powder. Giving a flavour of onions, it is used mainly in lentil dishes and in vegetarian cooking.

Amchur (Dry Mango Powder)

This tangy ingredient is the result of sun-dried green mangoes, which are then powdered. Rich in Vitamin C, amchur is used particularly to add a touch of sourness to a dish. It needs to be kept dry in storage, as it can get lumpy due to absorption of moisture.

Bay Laurel (Folia: *Laurus nobilis*) Tej Patta

Belonging to the avocado family (Lauraceae) it has its origins in Asia Minor and the Mediterranean. The leaf contains an important and volatile oil — cineol. Fresh leaves are bitter and the dried ones, if kept too long, lose their potency. The evergreen tree grows to a height of twenty metres. Its aromatic leaf is widely used in pickling, stews, soups, vinegars and curries. Most aromatic when dried, bay leaves are a vital part of a bouquet garni and useful for soups, stews and casseroles, as well as marinades for meat, fish and poultry. The famous leaves were used to crown Greek and Roman heroes centuries ago.

Chillies (*Capsicum annum*) Capsicum / Bell Peppers (*Capsicum frutescens*) Mirchi / Shimla Mirch

Chilli, like salt and pepper, is a universal spice which has transformed many a bland cuisine. It is used extensively by Latin America, Asia, Africa, the Caribbean and certain oriental cuisines. The term chilli is said to originate from the Mexican Indian word 'txile'. Native to Mexico, it was Christopher Columbus who took it to Europe, from where it spread to Africa, India and the Far East.

The flavour of the chilli is intoxicating to some, once the early sensations are overcome, and soon becomes an addiction. Rich in vitamin C, chillies stimulate the appetite and cool the body by creating sweat. Yoghurt is the best remedy to curb the burning sensation — not beer or water.

India being the largest producer and exporter, chillies are mass produced in Rajasthan and South India.

Capsicum, commonly called Shimla Mirch in India, is native to Central and South America and the West Indies. The hot sensation produced by capsicum is caused by a substance called capsaicin, which is concentrated in the membranes and seeds.

Paprika, a mild cousin, comes from the frutescens variety of chilli, and is used mainly for the colour it imparts to food.

Used in powder form, the membrane and seeds are mixed in. So named for its origins from Cayenne in French Guyana, it was introduced to India by Vasco da Gama in 1498 AD, and by 1560 it was flourishing in the Indian subcontinent. It is used as seasoning in biscuits, gravies and sauces.

Caraway Seeds (*Carum carui*) Ervadoce / Shia Jeera

They are the dried fruit of a biennial plant, native to northern Europe and are widely used on breads and in pork, liver and kidney-based dishes. Caraway is also the main ingredient of the liqueur, Kummel.

Cardamom (*Elettaria cardamomum*) Elaichi

This seed belongs to the ginger family (Zingiberaceae). The plant grows to a height of 2-5½ metres and is native to the evergreen forests of southern India, Sri Lanka and the Far East. The seeds retain their pleasant flavour if left in their pods, which are harvested before they ripen. Cardamom is extremely popular in the Middle East, where it is infused in coffee. The seed is widely used in Indian cuisine as it has a sharp pleasant flavour. In the Orient, it is a popular breath freshener. It is a common flavouring agent in rice, vegetable and baked dishes. Cardamom oil is used in the manufacture of perfumes and flavouring liqueurs.

Cinnamon (Cinnamomum verum, Cinnammum zeylandicum) Dalchini

In its wild state, the tree grows to a height of seventeen metres. When cultivated, it is grown to a height of 2½ metres. The spice is the bark of the tree, which is an unusual feature among spice plants. The bark is removed and the outer layer is stripped off. The strips are dried and curled to form quills which are pale brown in colour. Cinnamon and cassia are among the oldest spices known. The difference between the two is slight, with cinnamon being the better of the two in flavour and intensity.

True cinnamon has tightly rolled quills and is thinner than cassia. Cinnamon is native to southern India, Sri Lanka, Seychelles, Madagascar and the West Indies. Medicinally, cinnamon is used as a stimulant and a digestive. Apart from its use in apple pies and desserts, it is also an ingredient in pickles, chutneys, curries, pulaos and beverages, and in ground masalas.

Cassia (*Cinnamomum cassia*)

This is produced from Cinnamomum species other than *Cinnamomum verum* and is cultivated in China, Indonesia and Vietnam. Cassia is less intense in flavour than cinnamon.

Clove (*Eugenia caryophyllus*) Laung

The clove tree is an evergreen which originally grew in abundance in the Moluccas or Spice Islands. It was introduced to India and China early on and was well known in Europe by the Middle Ages. On flowering, the trees are covered in tiny red blossoms, which are then dried in the sun. India has now become the largest producer and exporter of cloves. This spice is often used whole to stud hams and roasts, and in the pickling of fruits and syrups. Cloves

are rich in essential oils, mainly eugenol, which are used in the manufacture of soaps, perfumes and toothpastes, and is an important spice in Indian masalas.

Coriander (*Coriandrum sativum*) Dhania

A perennial herb, it grows wild in southeast Europe, India and Morocco. To the Americans, coriander is known as cilantro. Another name is Chinese parsley. The leaves and stems have a pungent flavour, while the dried seeds are sweet and aromatic with a hint of bitterness. In Europe, it is also called dizzy corn owing to the narcotic effect it has on animals if eaten in large quantities. In India, it is one of the principal spices for seasoning fish and meat.

Cumin (*Cuminum cyminum*) Jeera

This spice, indigenous to the land of the Nile, is now grown in the Mediterranean islands, Morocco and India. Black cumin is grown and cultivated primarily in Iran, the Middle East and Kashmir. Cumin seed is pale brown when dried and like fennel and aniseed, it has a warm and lightly bitter taste. Mentioned in the Old and New Testaments, it was often referred to when calling a person a miser. Cumin was extensively used in Norman monasteries around 719 AD. In Indian cuisine, cumin is an important ingredient in meat dishes and ground masalas. In the coastal areas, it is widely used in fish preparations.

Curry Leaf (*Murraya keonigii*) Kari Patta

Kari patta belongs to the basil family and

grows wild in India. The leaf of this small plant lends a pungent and aromatic flavour to dishes. The curry leaf is widely used in Indian and Asian cooking.

Curry Powder
A unique blend of spices used predominantly in Indian cuisine. Curry powder is mainly added to curries and sauces for an enhanced flavour.

Dagad Phool / Kallupachi / Jeevanthi / Black Stone Flower / Sea Lichen
A rare dried flower, it is used largely in Chettinad cuisine, but is an ingredient of East Indian bottle masala, lending a sweet aromatic flavour. This lichen is actually a fungus from the Parmeliaceae family found on rocks and tree bark.

Fenugreek (*Trigonella foenum-graecum*) Methi
The origin of fenugreek lies within the eastern Mediterranean area. It has long been cultivated in India, the Mediterranean and North Africa. It is one of the oldest plants known to be cultivated. It is an annual herb (Leguminosae / Fabaceae), which grows to a height of about 90 cm. Its pods, about 8-15 cm long, give about ten to twenty oblong brownish seeds. It is rich in folic acid, which is essential for the formation of red blood cells and nucleic acid and had been used medicinally from ancient times. Fenugreek is widely used in salads and meat and fish dishes and curries. It has a strong flavour and is slightly bitter to taste; in some ways it is an acquired taste. Fenugreek leaves are eaten as a vegetable in many parts of the world.

Garlic (*Allium sativum*) Lasun
Garlic is an essential ingredient in most cuisines for its pungent and aromatic flavour. It features in the mythology and religious texts of several civilisations. The term garlic is from the Anglo Saxon 'garleac'. Garlic is a perennial herb related to the onion and is native to southern Europe and most countries with a warm climate. The bulb comprises flakes, which can number up to twenty. The bulbs are dried then plaited together and sold. There are various types of garlic, the most common being the white skinned variety. Pink or purple skinned garlic is much fleshier.

Garlic is indispensable in Asian and Mediterranean cooking. Strongest in its raw state, it takes on sweeter and milder tones when cooked. However, as it burns, it lends a bitter taste to a dish. It enhances the flavour of other ingredients.

Ginger (*Zingiber officinale*) Adrak
Ginger is the tuberous root of the plant which grows wild in the forests of South Asia and India. It belongs to the plant family, Zingiberaceae and is a perennial herb. It evolved in South East Asia. It is an underground tuberous stem, which constitutes the spice. India is the largest exporter of fresh, dried, ground and preserved ginger, as it is an important ingredient in Oriental cookery. It is a spice closely associated with the maintenance of good health. The Chinese and the Indians have long used ginger medicinally. It is widely used in chutneys, pickles, stewed fruit, pies, curries and cakes.

Ginger and garlic paste is often a base for gravies, as it is aromatic and lends a special flavour to a dish. The combination of ginger with cinnamon produces an unusual flavour in baked products. It is also crystallized in sugar. The essential oil, oleoresin is obtained from ginger.

Mace/ Nutmeg (*Myristica fragrans*) Javitri / Jaiphal

Nutmeg is the fruit of an evergreen tree, which grows to a height of four to ten metres. It is unique in that its fruit gives two flavours. Rich in vitamin A, mace is scarlet in colour and rich red-brown when dried. It is the outer covering of the seed. The nutmeg plant is native to the East Indies, the Moluccas and the Netherlands. Nutmeg was introduced to Eastern Europe in the twelfth century AD. Commercially, mace and nutmeg are used in sauces and confectionery products. However, both must be used in minute quantities, as they contain myristicin and elemicin, which are poisons.

Mint (*Mentha*) Pudina

Mint is a fragrant herb which grows in most parts of the world. It goes well with lamb, fruit-based desserts and cooling beverages. It is also an essential ingredient in the liqueur Crème de Menthe. Spearmint (*Mentha spicata*), which has slender, long delicate leaves, is preferred over peppermint (*Menthe piperata*) in cooking. Mint compliments aubergines and tomatoes.

Mixed Spice or Pickling Spice

A combination of whole spices such as cinnamon, cloves, cardamom, etc. pickling spice is used for pickling meats, fish, vegetables and relishes.

Pepper (*Piper nigrum*) Kali Mirch

Indigenous to the Malabar Coast of south-west India, pepper has its origins in the Western Ghats, and is one of the most widely used spices in the world. It has been in cultivation for over 3,000 years. The spice was carried to Java around 100 BC to 600 AD. Its qualities were well known to Europe by the Middle Ages. Around the Middle Ages, pepper was considered as currency more valuable than gold, and dowries, rents, etc. were paid in peppercorns. The vine is an evergreen plant and grows to a height of around four metres, which produces red berries 4-6 mm in diameter. The term pepper is from the Sanskrit word pippali, meaning berry.

The fruit is plucked and dried in the sun, leading to wrinkled black beads. Ripe berries are soaked in water to remove the outer skin and then dried in order to obtain white peppercorns, which are then ground to a fine powder. Medicinally, pepper is a stimulant and digestive, but is more in vogue as a seasoning. The spice is an important ingredient in the curing of Virginia-style hams, and in the making of pastrami. In India, it is essential in the preparation of rassam (pepper water). The pungency of pepper is due to alkaloids, which together with a volatile oil, constitute the sensory qualities of pepper.

Poppy Seeds (*Papaver rhoeas*) Khus-khus

The seed of the poppy plant, it is used in pickles, on breads, and in Indian cuisine as an important spice. The plant is native to Europe and the seeds are mostly imported from Holland.

Sesame Seeds (*Sesamum indicum*) Til

These seeds have a nutty flavour and are used in Indian cuisine, essentially in vegetarian dishes, and are sprinkled on Indian breads as a topping. The seeds are black or white, the oil comprising half the seed weight. Brought to the USA as 'benne' by African slaves, this seed is widely used for cooking, lighting and lubrication.

Star Anise (*Illicum verum*) Chakri Phool / Badiyan

Brought to India by Chinese traders centuries ago, it is also known as Chinese anise. The name, badiyan, is of Persian origin. It comes from an evergreen Chinese shrub of the magnolia family. Used extensively in Asian cuisine, this spice has a flavour that is a combination of hot liquorice and aniseed. Shaped like a star, its tiny brown seed in the centre is light brown and shiny. Apart from South Asian cuisine, it is widely used in Goan and Chettinad cuisine and is a main ingredient in spice powder mixes for its aromatic and health properties. One star added to stock or rice dishes lends a gamey flavour to a dish.

Tirphul (*Teppal*) Goa Spiceberry

This lesser know spice grows on a thorny tree called teppal in the regions of Goa and Karnataka, with tiny green berries which appear during the monsoons. These are collected and dried, upon which, the seeds open up to display tiny black seeds inside, which are removed and discarded; only the outer layer is used. Similar to Sichuan pepper by way of flavour, the spice is extensively used in the preparation of fish dishes and masalas.

Turmeric (*Curcuma longa*) Haldi

Native to India, China, Java and Peru, this plant is a member of the ginger family, Zingiberaceae. The mature roots of the plant are boiled, peeled and then dried. The dried root is then ground fine to a powder. Turmeric contains a yellow pigment known as cur cumin and is used as a cloth dye in Asia. Also used in cosmetics and medicines, its main use is in food. Turmeric is occasionally substituted as a cheaper version of saffron, although it has a different taste. The spice gives a warm, pleasant flavour with a hint of bitterness. It also plays an important role in the religious and marital customs of South Asia.

Terms and Meanings

A

Advent: The period of fasting and prayerful preparation before Christmas.

Aher cha Jevan: The first of the festive dinners on the eve of a wedding at the end of which prayers are offered for the repose of the souls of all the deceased in the family.

Aitolan: Cast iron pan for making sweets.

Amboshi: Dried and salted mango.

Amchur: Dried mango powder.

Aromatic: A plant, such as a herb or spice, that gives off a pleasing scent and is used to flavour food or drink.

B

Badam: (Amendoas) Almond.

Baida: (Avo) Egg.

Bain Marie: See double boiler.

Baingan: (Beringelas) Aubergine.

Bake Blind: Partially or fully bake a pie crust or shell. The pastry is lined with foil and filled with beans before baking to prevent it from rising up.

Bake: To cook by dry heat, usually in an oven.

Baked: (Refugada).

Baking Powder: (Fermento em po) A raising agent. Baked dishes containing baking powder should be allowed to stand for a few minutes allowing the leavening agents to work before being cooked in the oven.

Bangras: (Cavalas) Mackerel.

Barbecue: Is a loosely defined method of grilling over coal.

Barko: Embroidered motifs on dresses.

Baste or Mop: To moisten food while cooking with a liquid. This keeps the meat, and other foods, from drying out and encourages colour and flavour. A spoon, brush, bulb baster, or miniature mop can be used.

Batata: Potato.

Bâton: To cut vegetables into to ¼" x ¼" x 1½" to 2" strips.

Bay leaf: (Folhos de loura) Tej patta.

Béchamel: A basic white sauce of milk stirred into a roux of flour and butter, thickened, and flavoured with onion. This is also called by its Italian name, balsamella.

Bhakri: Thin rice breads.

Bhandaris: Toddy tappers.

Black-eyed Beans: (*Virvil lobia*).

Blanch: To plunge food briefly into boiling

water, and then into cold water to stop the cooking process. Blanching is used to loosen skins of fruits and vegetables, or to prepare them for further cooking by another method, and not to be confused with parboiling.

Blanching / Peeling Tomatoes: Score the top and bottom of the tomatoes with a sharp knife. Plunge into boiling water for a minute. Remove and put into cold water to stop the cooking. Peel the skin.

Blanching / Peeling Almonds: Boil some water and put the almonds into it. Leave for a while, then remove the skins.

Bombil: Bombay duck (*harpadontidae galatinous*), a soft glutinous fish found in the Arabian Sea.

Bouquet Garni: Herbs tied together, placed in a cheesecloth bundle or put in an infuser. This allows the herbs to be removed easily from food before it is served. The classic bouquet garni has thyme, parsley and bay leaf.

Brahmins: The upper classes in the caste hierarchy.

Brain: (Miolhos) beja.

Braise: A method in which food is first browned, and then cooked in a tightly covered pan or oven, with a small amount of liquid. It is cooked at low heat for a long period of time.

Bran: 10 g of bran produces 2 g of fibre. It is the coarse outer layer of most cereal grains, which is removed during the early stages of milling. It is the best known source of dietary fibre.
15 g of rice = 3.8 g of fibre;
10 g of wheat = 4.5 g of fibre.

Breadcrumbs: (Migalhas). Toast bread in an oven but do not brown it, then crush it.

Bread: Pao.

Broil: To cook food directly under or over a heat source, usually in the oven under the top broiling element or on the grill.

Broth: A flavourful liquid made by simmering meat, poultry or seafood in water. Broths and stocks are virtually the same thing. The word 'stock' simply implies that it is being saved (stocked) for another preparation, such as a sauce or soup. Broth should stand on its own and be ready to serve.

Brown Stock: A broth made by browning the main ingredients (usually meat, meat bones, or poultry) on the stove or in the oven, before adding liquid.

Browning Onions: The regular way of browning onions is to heat oil in a pan and fry thinly sliced onions till brown. Before browning, the sliced onions are sprinkled over with salt and left aside for 10 minutes. The water is then squeezed out and the onions left to drain on kitchen paper.

Butter: (Manteiga) Maska, makkhan.

C

Cabbage: (Repolho) Bandgobi.

Cake: (Bole).

Capsicum: (Pimento) Bell pepper, Shimla mirch.

Caramelisation: All meat and vegetables contain some sugar (in the form of carbohydrates). Under intense dry heat, as in roasting or sautéing, these sugars break down. The result is a brown colour and rich flavour called caramelisation.

Cauliflower: (Couveflor) Phoolgobi.

Celery: (Aipo).

Cereals: The term derives itself from Ceres the Roman goddess of harvests and corn. They consist of edible grass seeds. The cultivation of cereals marked a transition from hunting to agriculture. There is archaeological evidence that wheat was cultivated between 15,000 to 10,000 BC. Primarily being wheat and barley, it spread from Egypt and the Middle East to Greece and Rome and from there to Britain, India and Far East Asia. Rice became the staple food of India and Far East Asia, while rye and oats were the staple diet in northern Europe.

Chamars: Shoemakers.

Chapatti: Originated in India with a long history, it is a fine example of primitive bread, which is unleavened. Indigenous to different continents, such as the Ethiopian injera and Mexican tortillas. A staple in the diet, it is very often broken and used to scoop up gravies. Made with wheat flour known as atta, it was originally ground with a mortar and pestle.

Chauvnies: Small earthenware cups for consuming alcohol, like khimad.

Chaval: (Arroz) Rice.

Cheese: (Queijo).

Cherry: (Bilimbi).

Chicken: (Galinha) Murghi.

Chiffonade: Literally, this means 'made of rags'. It refers to thin strips of vegetables and herbs. Several leaves are staked on top of each other and rolled tightly like a cigar. Thin slices are made across the leaves while holding the roll tightly.

Chinal: Leather sandal.

Chop: There are four separate 'chopping' dimensions, from rough chop (any large and regular sizes), to coarse chop, chop, then the smallest, mince.

Chundri: Silk or cotton scarf or head covering.

Clay oven: (Forma).

Clove: (Cravos) Laung.

Coconut: (Coco) Nariyal.

Condiment: An aromatic mix, such as pickles, chutneys and some sauces and relishes, that accompanies food. Usually kept on the table throughout the main service.

Conjee: (Peile) Rice water.

Coriander: (Cilantro) Kothmir, hara dhania.

Cornflour: (Maisena).

Croquettes: Cooked food, moulded into cylindrical shapes, coated with egg and breadcrumbs and deep-fried.

Cumin: (Cominho) Jeera.

D

Dalchini: (Canela) Cinnamon.

Dals: (Lentilha) Lentils.

Deep-fry: To immerse food completely into hot fat at 140°C-190°C.

Dhakti Sakhar: A preliminary engagement. An auspicious ceremony between both parties prior to a marriage, with sugar playing an integral part. A preliminary gesture to the formal engagement.

Dhobis: Laundrymen.

Dice: There are at least four different sized dices:
brunoise — $\frac{1}{8}"x\frac{1}{8}"$;
concassée (small dice) — ¼"x¼";
medium dice — $\frac{1}{3}"x\frac{1}{3}"$; and
large dice — ¾"x¾"

Dole: Chain with seven gold and seven coral beads.

Double boiler: A larger pan with water in it, and a smaller pan inserted above the water. The water is then simmered, warming or cooking the ingredients in the smaller inserted pan. It is recommended that one finds a glass double boiler, for the obvious reason: that one can tell when to add more water.

Dowry: Dagina.

Dredge: To coat food lightly with flour, corn meal or breadcrumbs, to enhance the browning or deep-frying.

Duledi: Six chains of small gold beads.

E

Elaichi: (Cardomomo) Cardamom.

F

Fat / lard: (Gordura).

Fenugreek: (Fenacho) Methi.

Fish: (Peixe) Macchi.

Flour: (Farinha) Atta.

Fold: To combine one mixture with another through repeated gentle turning-over motions — not beating or stirring — to keep the air inside.

Forcemeat: A mixture of finely ground, raw or cooked meat, poultry, fish, vegetables or fruit, mixed with breadcrumbs and various seasonings.

G

Garma: Brass dining plate.

Gauri cha Jevan: A wedding dinner of the Koli community to which only married women were invited prior to the wedding.

Gharat: Grinding stones.

Ghee: Clarified butter.

Ginger: (Gengibre) Adrak.

Glazing: This term has two meanings: 1. subjecting a roast of meat to high heat and basting it until a glistening, golden brown crust is formed. The meat glaze is purely a stock which is reduced to a glutinous consistency. With the proper infusion of cream or butter, a glaze can be used as a sauce.

2. Coating pastries and cakes with an icing.

Grate: Cut foods such as cheese or cabbage into shreds, flakes or tiny particles using a tool with sharp-edged holes, a knife or a food processor.

Grilling: Using a grill. There are two types of grilling: direct and indirect. Direct cooking is grilling without the lid, and directly over a live fire at 250°C to 375°C. This is usually used for large pieces of meat, chicken or vegetables, and imparts a tasty caramelisation. The fire itself can be very hot on one side, and cooler on the other. Indirect grilling, as its name implies, grills, or more properly, bakes, at the opposite side of the grill where no coal is located. The vents under the coal and above the food are open. Often, smoking is done in a variation of the indirect grilling process.

H

Ham (leg): (Perna / Presunta).

Hamlets: Pakhadis.

Herb / spice: A herb is the leafy portion of an aromatic plant; a spice is practically every other part of that plant, i.e. the bark, root, etc.

Hydrogenated fat: It is made by treating liquid oils like corn oil with hydrogen.

I

Ice bath: A pan containing iced water. Used to cool foods rapidly.

Incorporate: To mix thoroughly.

Infusion: A hot liquid for steeping herbs and flavourings like spices and peel. The extraction of flavour from a food in a hot liquid (below the boiling point). Usually refers to teas and coffees, but can also apply to cooking.

J

Jaggery: Unrefined sugar, gud.

Janthar: Public / guests.

Joint: Cutting of game and poultry along its joints.

Julienne: Foods that are cut into $1/_{16}"x1/_{16}"x1½"-2"$ strips. Or vegetables cut into thin matchstick-sized strips.

K

Kajota: Silver girdle worn by Koli men.

Kakdi: (Cenoura) Cucumber.

Kanayadan: Giving away ceremony of the bride to the groom prior to the wedding. Performed by the parents before the altar of the house.

Kanda: (Cebola) Onion.

Kanji: (Canji) Boiled rice water.

Karela: (Caratins) Bitter Gourd.

Kastyache: A nine to ten yard sari worn by the Samvedi, Nesana and Vadval women.

Kekda: (Carangue jos) Crab.

Khapri: Flat clay dish for baking.

Khatris: Native to the district of Thane, Sopara.

Khumbars: Potters.

Koitha: Cleaver.

Kolbi: (Camerao) Prawn.

Koli: Fisher community living along the coastal areas. Their origins can be traced to the migratory tribes who came from the Balaghat and the Mahadev hills and settled along the coast. (Mahadeo Kolis, Malhar Kolis, Dhor Kolis.)

Kolivadas: Hamlets of the fisher community.

Kubudor: Steamer.

Kunbis: Farmers and cultivators.

Kupta: Earthen jar for heating liquor.

L

Lal Bhopla: (Abobora) Red pumpkin, kaddu

Larding: This process enhances the flavour of rather bland cuts of meat. Here, strips of fat or bacon are drawn through the meat with a larding needle.

Lasun: (Alhos) Garlic.

Lent: The period of fasting and prayerful preparation before Easter.

Liaison: Binding or thickening of soup or sauce by means of egg yolk, blood, or starch such as flour (see roux), arrowroot, corn starch, or tapioca.

Limbo: (Limao) Lemon or lime, nimbu.

Liver: (Figado).

Lobster: (Lagosta).

Lugade: A nine-yard sari worn by Koli women.

M

Maas: (Bife) Beef.

Macaroni: Macarrao.

Macerate: To soak ingredients into a liquid, usually alcohol (macerate usually applies to fruits) or in flavoured liquid. Also, when a saline solution is added, the purpose of which is to draw out water.

Mandap: Pavilion or area prepared for special occasions.

Marinade: A liquid, including seasonings and acid (vinegar, citrus or wine) in which food is steeped before cooking, in order to flavour it. Marinating does not actually make the meat tender. To do so would seriously alter the texture of the meat and make it unpleasant. Food marinated with cornflour (e.g. meat, prawns) should have oil added to avoid it sticking in a lump.

Marinate: This is the most popular method for flavouring meat using a variety of ingredients and allowing them to marry for a couple of hours.

Marrow: A soft, fatty tissue found in the hollow centre of an animal's bone, particularly in the shin and leg bones. Also a vegetable.

Masala: A powdered mix of spices or herbs. There are two types of masalas — dry and wet. Traditionally all masalas are hand-pounded and hand-ground.

Mestizos (of mixed blood): Offspring of unions between the Portuguese and locals.

Millet: Used for brewing and for food since prehistoric times, in Asia, Africa and Europe. It travelled from Europe to Arabia, the Persian Gulf and to India, where it has been grown since 2000 BC, and to China, following the Silk Route.

Milling: The mechanical processing of grinding, cracking, and / or removing the hull, bran, or germ from wholegrains.

Mince: To cut in very small pieces, or grind fine.

Mirchi: (Malangueta) chilli.

Mirepoix: A mix of vegetables like carrot, leek, celery and onion used to flavour stocks, etc. and to season sauces, soups and stews. It is also used as a bed to braise meats and fish.

Mise en place: Literally this means 'put in place'. It requires one to thoroughly read the recipe, and then organise all the ingredients, equipment and serving pieces prior to cooking

Moti Sakhar / Sakhar Puda: A ritual of the formal engagement when the boy came of age to be married. Called Sakhar Puda by the Vadvals and the Salcette Christians.

Moya: The shaving ceremony of the groom by a family member on the eve of the wedding, following which a gold ring is presented to the bride and the groom, by the parents.

N

Navalchaya Vidhi: A ceremony performed by the Samvedi Christian community in which the bride was adorned in all her new jewellery.

Nhavis: Barbers.

Non-reactive: In cooking, any non-porous material that won't react (by discolouring or changing the taste) with acidic foods. This includes glass, stainless steel, glazed ceramic and enamel.

Nutmeg: (Noz-moscada) Jaiphal.

O

Oblique: To cut vegetables so that all sides are oblique to the opposing side.

Oil: (Oleo) Tael.

Oxidation: A chemical reaction that occurs when a substance is exposed to oxygen. The oxygen reacts with elements in the substance to change it, as when cut apples turn brown.

Oyster: Ostras.

P

Pan-frying: To pan-fry, one gives a gentler treatment to the food, as opposed to sautéing. In comparing pan-frying to sautéing, pan-frying occurs when one uses about ¼" of fat or oil and cooks over moderate to moderate to high heat. It leaves the food relatively undisturbed, except for an occasional flip or turn with a spatula, fork, or tongs. Choose large pieces of food and those that are coated with bread before cooking, such as thick pork chops, bone-in chicken pieces and whole trout. Fats with a high smoke point, like vegetable oil or lard, are very traditional fats for pan-frying.

Parada: Earthen jars for storing wheat.

Parboil: Partial cooking of food in boiling or simmering liquid. Similar to blanching, but the cooking time is longer.

Pata: Grinding stone for wet masalas.

Peas and Beans (Dried): Soak in water overnight, or for a few hours before use.

Peppercorn: (Pimenta) Kalamiri, kali mirch.

Peroz: Three chains with large gold beads.

Phadke: White shawl worn by Koli women.

Piercing: Foods which have a skin like apples, potatoes or tomatoes, need piercing when being baked whole.

Pies: (Empada).

Pinda: Low stool used while eating.

Pith: The soft, white membrane that lies between the peel and the pulp of a citrus fruit. It has a bitter flavour, and when trying to extract the zest, i.e. the skin of a citrus, one avoids incorporating the pith.

Poach: To cook food gently in hot liquid just below the boiling point. Liquids can vary from broths, to water and syrups.

Poppy Seeds: (Semente de paposa) Khus-khus.

Pounding: A method practised for years. Done to break down the connective meat tissues and release the juices. These juices must be retained in the meat with the help of flour, or much flavour is lost.

Prepared Vegetables: Vegetables which are cut, chopped, grated as specified in a recipe.

Puri: Traditionally a peasant bread of Georgia. A long thin loaf, it is baked in an oven known as a tone, very similar to the tandoor oven of north India. The dough is based on a starter, a method which has been handed down through the generations. In India, it is a flat disc, which is deep-fried. The puri in India was considered the food of the wealthy as it required oil and heavy utensils to prepare.

R

Ramekin: A straight-sided baking dish, used for soufflés and baked custards.

Reduce: To boil a liquid till its volume is reduced by evaporation. This thickens the liquid and intensifies the flavours. So season a reduction after it is made, not before.

Refresh: To submerge cooked food in cold water to cool it quickly and stop further cooking. It is also known as shocking.

Reheating: Foods being reheated must be steaming and hot to the touch.

Resting: Heat drives meat juices from the surface when cooking. Allowing meat to rest before slicing, lets these juices seep back towards the surface.

Rice: Oriza sativa. Legend has it that rice was consumed in China around 5,000 years ago. Marking the beginning of the sowing season, Emperor Shen would plant the first and best rice seeds, followed by his sons who then planted different varieties, a custom followed to this day. Influenced by Confucius, most Chinese prefer white rice to others. In those days, the husk was used for polishing gems. Rice arrived in Egypt around the fourth century BC. At about the same time, India was exporting it to Greece. Rice plays a vital role in religious rites around the world. In Japan, innumerable shrines line country roads dedicated to Inari, the rice god. Samurais, the emperor's warriors, were paid in rice. In China, coolies, the labourers, were also paid in rice. At weddings, rice is sprinkled over the bridal couple as a symbol of fertility.

Roast: (Assada).

Roti: (Apa) Indian flatbread.

S

Sada: Half-sari worn by girls.

Saivar ceremony: The tossing of flower petals into the well to appease the water fairies.

Sakkar: (Acucar) Sugar.

Salcette Christians: Upper-class Christians who had the benefits of a Western education came to be known as Salcette Christians. Mainly Prabhus, Brahmins, Khatris and Sonars, an ethnic minority converted by the Franciscans and Jesuit missionaries between 1547 and 1600.

Salt: (Sal) Namak. Add salt at the final stage or after cooking as it draws moisture out of foods. It is sodium chloride, irrespective of its origins, i.e. whether from the seas or a mine. The crystals come in various shapes and have some differences. How they act and react with various foods becomes a matter of importance to cooking.

• Garlic salt is a unique combination of fresh garlic and salt. It is used to flavour sauces, tomato juice and a variety of vegetable dishes.

• Kosher salt is an additive-free, coarse-grained salt. Of course, Jews use it in their cooking, but it is also often used by chefs, who prefer it because of the 'feel' of the quantity and its slowness to melt.

• Onion salt is a combination of freshly chopped onion and salt. This is then dried and bottled. Onion salt gives a mild onion flavour to dishes, namely salads.

• Pickling salt is a fine-grained salt used to make brines for pickles, sauerkraut, etc. It contains no additives, which would cloud the brine.

• Rock salt has a greyish cast because it is not as refined as other salts, which means it retains more minerals and harmless impurities. It comes in chunky crystals and is used predominantly as a bed on which to serve baked oysters and clams and to combine with ice to make ice cream in crank-style ice-cream makers.

• Sea salt is the type used down through the ages and is the result of the evaporation of sea water — the more costly of the two processes. It comes in fine-grained or larger crystals. It's understandable that, for cooking, the texture and melting properties of certain salts is important, basically for taste. Remember, it is more potent than normal table salt.

- Seasoned salt is regular salt combined with other flavouring, ingredients, examples being onion salt, garlic salt and celery salt. Salt substitutes contain no sodium.
- Sour salt, also called citric salt, is extracted from acidic fruits, such as lemons and limes. It is used to add tartness to traditional dishes.
- Table salt is a fine-grained salt with additives that make it free-flowing and is mainly used in cooking and as a table condiment. Iodised salt is table salt with added iodine (sodium iodide) which is particularly important in areas that lack natural iodine, an important preventative for hypothyroidism.

Salted: (Salgada)

Samvedi Christians: Residents of the northern areas of Bassein, with close proximity to the Vaitarna river. Brahmin by origin.

Sari Choli: A ceremony performed by the Samvedi Christian community. The presentation of a new sari to the bride.

Sarpatel: A dish made using all the leftover parts of the pig. Unlike the Goan recipe, it is not made with a wet, ground masala.

Sausage: (Churico).

Sauté: In French, sauté means, 'to jump'. That describes the method in which food is cooked quickly in a small amount of butter or oil. The food 'jumps' as it is either rapidly stirred or shaken over the heat. (See pan-frying and stir-fry.)

To sauté, one uses only the smallest amount of fat or oil — enough to lightly coat the bottom of the pan and prevent the food from sticking.

It is done on moderate-high to high heat — hot enough to make the food sizzle, sputter, and even jump a little the instant it hits the pan. Keep the food in nearly constant motion, by stirring with a spoon or actually flipping the pan, so that it browns evenly. Choose fast-cooking foods for sautéing, i.e. cutlets, vegetable pieces, shrimp. Use fats such as clarified butter, vegetable oil, or a mix of butter and oil.

Scald: To heat milk almost to boiling point — just till tiny bubbles begin to form around the inside edge of the pan.

Score: Make shallow or deep cuts in a decorative pattern with a sharp knife. Ham fat is often scored in diamond shapes. You score the thickest part of whole fish with 2-3 slashes so that part will cook as fast as the thin areas.

Seal: To fry meat over high heat, thus preventing the juices from escaping.

Seasoning: Salt and pepper.

Seasoning a Pan: To coat a pan or other metal cooking surface (not non-stick) with oil and then heat it repeatedly and wipe off excess oil. This produces a clean and non-stick surface.

Semolina: (Semola de trigo) Sooji, rava.

Shenga: (Moringueiro) A vegetable called drumstick, Sujjan ka phalli.

Shewli: (Ameijoas) Clams.

Shiran (big): Chain with eight gold beads interspersed with coral beads.

Shiran (small): Chain with five gold and five coral beads.

Short Crust Pastry: Used as a base for

pie bases, crusts, tart shells and barquettes.

Shred: Cut or grate into long, even, thin strands.

Simmer: To cook food just below boiling point.

Snake Gourd: (Podolim) Chirchinda.

Sonars: Goldsmiths.

Soop: Fan-shaped basket for removing chaff from wheat.

Soup: (Sopa).

Soy Sauce: This extremely important ingredient in Asian cooking is a dark, salty sauce made by fermenting boiled soybeans and roasted wheat or barley. Although there is essentially one main type of soy sauce, China and Japan produce a number of varieties ranging in colour from light to dark and in texture from thin to very thick.

Spillage: Always use a pan larger than the quantity of food to avoid food spilling over.

Standing Food: A golden rule to remember is that food cooks even after the oven is turned off. Allow food to stand for a while if consuming immediately.

Steam: Cook on a rack above (never touching) boiling liquid, in a covered container.

Steep: Soak a food item such as tea, herbal leaves or saffron in liquid that is just under the boiling point, to soften the food or flavour the liquid.

Stew: Cook food slowly in a simmering, well-seasoned liquid in a covered pan.

Stir-fry: Sauté small, uniform-sized pieces of food quickly over high heat, often in a wok or skillet, tossing the food constantly.

Stirring: Stir food from outside in to ensure even heating. Cooking time and food quantity should be in proportion. When cooking large portions of food, stir the food at short intervals to allow even cooking.

Stock: A more or less gelatinous and aromatic liquid, prepared by poaching meat, fish, or bones in water or more stock. Virtually the same as a broth or bouillon, except that these terms imply that the liquid will be served as is, whereas stock implies eventual use in another preparation. (See broth, brown stock, white stock.)

Stock Clarification: In a pan, add the stock. Whisk egg white and stir it in. Cook to a boil and simmer for 5 minutes. The egg will coagulate and clarify the stock. Strain and set aside.

Strain: Place food in a sieve to separate liquid from solids, or force soft food through a sieve to purée it and remove hard particles.

Suckling: (Leitao) Piglet.

Suet: Beef fat.

Sutars: Those in managerial and supervisory positions came to be known as such.

Sweat: When foods, usually vegetables, are cooked over low heat in a small amount of fat (usually butter), drawing out juices to remove rawness and develop flavour. Frequently parchment paper is placed on top of the vegetables, to help hold in the juices.

T

Taluka: District.

Tamarind: Fruit of a tall shade tree, native to Asia and North Africa. The large brown pods contain small seeds and sweet-sour pulp. This pulp is a common flavouring in Indian and Middle Eastern cuisines. Use like lemon juice.

Tava: A griddle or cast iron flat pan for roasting spices and chapattis.

Temper: To add slowly a hot liquid to eggs or other foods to gradually raise their temperature without making them curdle.

Tempering: With reference to Indian cooking, tempering or tadka refers to cooking spices in oil before or after a dish is prepared. When done, it is poured hot over the cooked food.

Time: Always use the lowest cooking time specified in your recipe.

Tipree: Dry ingredient measure, round cylindrical unit, 350 cubic cm.

Toddy: (Seiva de palmeira) Fermented liquor of the palm tree.

Tomato: (Tomate) Tamatar.

Tomato paste: Tomatoes that have been cooked for several hours and strained, then reduced to a thick concentrate. Used for thickening, flavouring and colour. When used as a base, where the paste is heated in a heavy-bottomed pan, keeping the heat no higher than moderate, and stirring it constantly, the results are quite astonishing! The browning of the paste turns starch to sugar, develops depths of flavour, and adds rich colour and aroma to all savoury cooking.

Tomato purée: Tomatoes that have been briefly cooked and strained. Used as a thickener.

Truss: To sew or tie around meat or poultry after stuffing.

Umbracha Pani: Well water. Also a part of the wedding ceremony where young unmarried girls with pots tiered on their heads and accompanied by lanterns, singing and dancing, proceed to a well to draw the water which is then used by the bridal couple to bathe.

V

Vadval Christians: Residents of the southern part of Bassein. Their origins lie within the Pachkalshis and Somvanshi Kshatriya (warrior) class.

Vanilla: Baunilha.

Vinegar: (Vinaigre) Sirca.

Volvani: A ceremony to ward off the evil eye by circling a coin over the head of the bride or groom to be.

W

Wadi: Small collective huts, little cottages and bungalows.

Water Bath: Small dishes are placed in a larger pan. Boiling water is then poured around the dishes into the larger pan, creating a variation on a double boiler.

Wheat: As with other cereals, milling influences its nutritive value. Originating in the Valley of the Tigris around 7000 BC, it spread to Asia Minor to Egypt and Europe. Ancient civilisations of the Middle East used it as a staple grain, especially for porridge. Wheat germ is the husk, which is removed during milling. 10 g of husk produce 2 g of fibre.

Wedding Banns: Official public announcement in the church regarding forthcoming marriage and seeking registration of objections if any.

Wedding Sari: The traditional red silk sari

enriched with gold embroidery.

Whip: Incorporate air into a mixture by beating.

Whisk: Beat to mix, using a whisk.

White Stock: A stock made by adding liquid directly to meat, seafood, or vegetables, without browning the ingredients first. White stocks are used when a clear, very pale liquid is required.

Wine: (Vinho).

Y

Yogurtor / curd: Yogurt is made by inoculating partially evaporated milk with a fermenting bacterium (*Lactobacillus bulgaricus*) which thickens the milk.

Yeast: There are many fungi, some good and some bad. The ones which interest us are better known as sugar fungi. This is mainly due to their ability to digest glucose and produce alcohol, carbon dioxide and energy. These microscopic organisms have the ability to live without the presence of oxygen. Yet, in order to multiply, they require oxygen. The addition of warm water at 37°C and sugar provides the elements required for them to feed. Yeast activates at 27°C-37°C at room temperature. On mixing into the dough, yeast moves into an anaerobic stage. It still lives, but lacks the ability to reproduce. Hence, it produces carbon dioxide, which expands, filling up the air pockets in the dough — the air that has been incorporated while kneading. Dough on being kneaded well, has finer air pockets leading to a smoother texture in the final product. Temperatures are important for yeast. Yeast can survive low temperatures but get killed when the centre of the dough or loaf reaches about 52°C. Salt retards yeast action.

Z

Zest: The outer skin of citrus fruits where the essential oils are concentrated. The French word is zeste, not to be confused with ziste, the white pith beneath the outer layer of skin.

Zopadis: Small huts or tenements

Weights and Measures

Old Indian	Pound	Metric
1 tola	2.5 oz	10 g
1 chittak	2 oz	56.7 g
1 pau	8 lb	226.8 g
1 seer (4 paus)	2 lb	907.2 g
1 pailee (4 seers)	8 lb	3.629 kg
1 maund (14 seers)	28 lb	12.700 kg
1 phara (16 pailees)	128 lb	58.060 kg
1 Tipree (Measure, 350 cubic cm.)		

Conversions
Fahrenheit To Centigrade: Subtract 32, multiply by 5, divide by 9.
Centigrade To Fahrenheit: Multiply by 9, divide by 5, add 32.

Index